BASKETS AS TEXTILE ART

BASKETS AS TEXTILE ART

ED ROSSBACH

Sponsored by the American Crafts Council

VAN NOSTRAND REINHOLD COMPANY
New York   Cincinnati   Toronto   London   Melbourne

CREDITS Figure 3: Collection of Sky-Yello Institute, Auburn, California.

Figures 10, 11, 27, 74, 169, 206, and 207: Collection of American Museum of Natural History.

Figures 12, 14, 16, 17, 26, 33, 34, 35, 36, 37, 39, 40, 41, 42, 43, 44, 45, 46, 47, 49, 50, 51, 54, 55, 58, 59, 67, 79, 82, 83, 86, 88, 90, 94, 95,103,105,106,110,112,113, 114, 116, 120, 121, 122, 124, 125, 128, 130, 132, 156, 163, 171, 172, 174, 175, 177, 178, 181, 188, 189, 192, 208, 217, 218, 223, and 226: Collection of Robert H. Lowie Museum of Anthropology, University of California, Berkeley.

Figures 19, 20, 61, 78, 87, 93, 109, 131, 136, 137, 138, 155, 180, 183, 221, and 222: Collection of Department of Anthropology, University of California, Davis.

Figures 60, 72, 75, 76, 77, 81, 168, 191, and 204: Collection of Lea van P. Miller.

Figure 154: Collection of Louise Barco Allrich.

Remaining figures, unless otherwise credited: Collection of the author.

Color plates 2, 5, 6, 7, 8, 9, 10, 11, 15, 17, 18, 19, and 20: Collection of Robert H. Lowie Museum of Anthropology, University of California, Berkeley.

Color plates 6, 9, 11, and 18: Photographs by Lia Cook.

Van Nostrand Reinhold Company Regional Offices:
New York Cincinnati Chicago Millbrae Dallas
Van Nostrand Reinhold Company International Offices:
London Toronto Melbourne

Copyright © 1973 by Litton Educational Publishing, Inc.
Library of Congress Catalog Card Number 73-1628
ISBN 0-442-27049-6

Designed by Rosa Delia Vasquez

Published by Van Nostrand Reinhold Company
450 West 33rd Street, New York, N.Y. 10001

16 15 14 13 12 11 10 9 8 7 6 5 4 3 2 1

To my wife

ACKNOWLEDGMENTS

I am indebted to the University of California for sponsoring my research related, one way or another, to basketry. I gratefully acknowledge use of the libraries and collections on the Berkeley and Davis campuses. Over a long period of time I had easy access to the extensive basket collection of the Lowie Museum of Anthropology, and the help of Senior Museum Anthropologist Lawrence E. Dawson, whose familiarity with the Museum's resources, and with basketry construction and materials, is so enviable. The Library Service Photographic Laboratory gave excellent service in printing my negatives. Of immeasurable value was my long association with Berkeley's outstanding textile faculty. Most especially I wish to acknowledge my debt to Lea van P. Miller. I am grateful too to my students whose enthusiasms and valuations were supportive to my own work in most subtle ways.

I thank all those who permitted me to use photographs, and who lent me baskets to study and photograph, and who gave me baskets. The American Museum of Natural History allowed me access to their collection of Andaman Island baskets, and to their large photograph file.

I thank Lois Moran of the American Crafts Council for her encouragement and assistance in presenting my manuscript; and Lois Ladas, Paul Smith, and Lee Nordness for their positive responses to my basketmaking. Most of all I thank my wife.

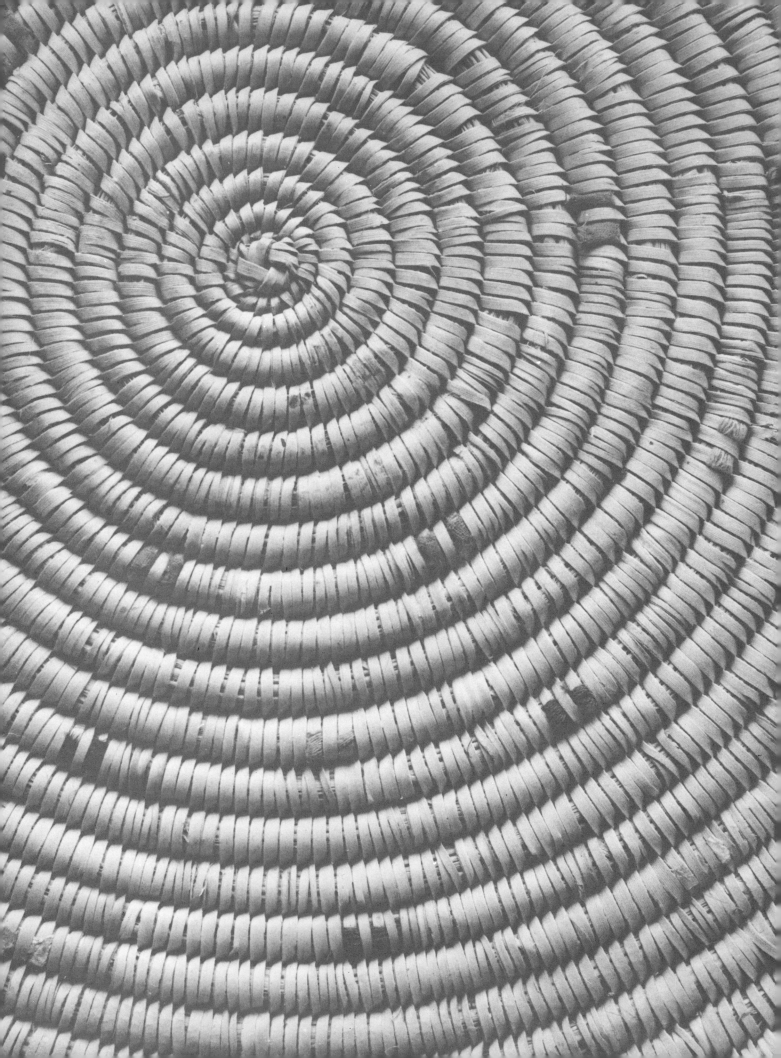

CONTENTS

INTRODUCTION

In the Aleutian Islands during the war I tried to make my first basket. The isolated turbulent land seemed to discourage any way of human life, even the army's way of superimposing and sustaining life from without. Yet I knew that the Aleuts had survived there. The most obvious resource was the plant life, which the Aleuts had used for baskets. I set about gathering individual grasses and stalks which seemed promising although I had little idea what constituted quality in basketry materials. No information was available, for the Aleuts had been removed from their islands and, strangely, nothing of their culture was to be seen anywhere. It was as though hostile elements had furiously erased every mark of human existence and returned the land to something primeval, alien, and—despite the army which had alighted—uninhabited. In wandering over the soggy tundra during the long months I observed the plants and birds, the mists and rainbows, and occasionally the precise forms of distant volcanoes rising in perfect cones from the ocean which lay on all sides. I found myself indulging in a solitary ritual of observation. The islands became for me, at least in retrospect, a land of dreams—various, beautiful, and new. I achieved no baskets, only a box of selected grasses and a brittle start of interweaving.

Since then I have paid attention to Aleutian baskets. Through watching an Aleut basketmaker at work I became aware, most of all, that the traditional process requires time and a stable existence, one season to the next, and a general sense of the appropriateness of the activity to the total life. Certain grasses at certain times of year, selected and sorted according to certain standards, worked at certain seasons in certain moist atmospheres according to certain techniques, into certain forms with certain decorations, for certain purposes.

When I again tried to make baskets many years later, I had acquired some knowledge of textile fibers and techniques. With examples and instructions at hand, and purchased materials, I was able to produce amateurish results. Yet I continue to value the Aleutian experience, with the insight it gave me into the nature of basketmaking as something related to a place and a way of life.

In searching for information about baskets I discovered that little attention has been paid them. I began to feel that they were being slighted. The scant literature on baskets suggests a wave of such feeling during the early years of this century as part of the arts and crafts movement and the protest against a too-exclusive view of what constituted fine art. In those remarkable years when anthropological expeditions were desperately active throughout the world describing the material cultures of the remaining primitive peoples, the traditional Indian crafts in the United States were seen to be dying. Those which still existed were already degenerate. The old work was rated as vastly superior. Attempts were made to search out, preserve, and perpetuate. Nothing appeared quite so hopeless then as it does today. The possibility still seemed to exist that something regarding the traditional handcrafts might change for the better.

In 1901, as part of the interest in crafts early in the century, George Wharton James published his work on Indian basketry to aid collectors and to stimulate interest in Indians, whom he had been studying for many years. James is described as a man of hobbies, enthusiasms, and sympathies, rather than a scholar or an artist. From Pasadena, California, he edited a publication entitled *The Basket, The Journal of the Basket Fraternity or Lovers of Indian Baskets and Other Good Things.*

James acknowledged his debt to Otis Tufton Mason, who was to become head curator of anthropology in the Smithsonian Institution. Mason's papers had for years appeared in its reports. In 1904 he published them as a book, calling it, significantly, *Indian Basketry, Studies in a Textile Art Without Machinery.*

Like William Morris, both James and Mason valued the hand product—and more specifically the *traditional* hand product. They were concerned about the deplorable design of machine-made useful objects, and the destruction of the individual craftsman. James regarded the baskets of the modern civilized world as rude commercialism, "ugly and homely," tolerated only for their usefulness. To him the fine Indian baskets were "wickerwork masterpieces—poems, paintings, sculpture, cathedrals, music"—that is, fine art. In his turn, Mason decried "the cheap patented ware made from veneering which threatened to obliterate the ancient plicated basket." He wanted basketry exalted as a pastime and a fine art. And like James, he hoped his book would stimulate not only an appreciation of baskets, but a humane feeling for the Indian women who made them.

While Indians were urged to continue their traditional basketmaking, the American public was encouraged to learn the craft. Simple how-to-do-it manuals appeared. They are still among the basketry books in our public libraries. Basketry was featured as a serious educational endeavor. Some authors no longer stressed the utilitarian aspects of basketry but were anxious to perpetuate the craft as an "art." The most appealing monograph was an act of love called *Raffia Basketry as a Fine Art,* published in Deerfield, Massachusetts, in 1915. The book is all high ideals, dedication, and sentiment. Its message is of happiness in weaving baskets while the scent of flowers comes in the windows and the squirrels chatter in the elm boughs.

This self-conscious effort to turn the Deerfield baskets into art resulted in the abandonment of the geometric patterns so natural to basketry in favor of a rather painterly representationalism. The baskets became a surface for realistic interpretations, like paintings in colored raffia. Curiously, the bottoms continued to show the traditional geometric patterning. The shapes of the baskets were treated as of secondary interest. Now, half a century later, these Deerfield baskets recall the decorated surfaces of hand-painted china on plate-rails, and the glass lampshades with their illuminated sunsets. In trying to become an art consonant with contemporary views, basketry approached painting, just as tapestry had traditionally done—and indeed it is this quality in tapestry which, unfortunately, still makes it generally considered as the textile art most worthy of a place among the fine arts.

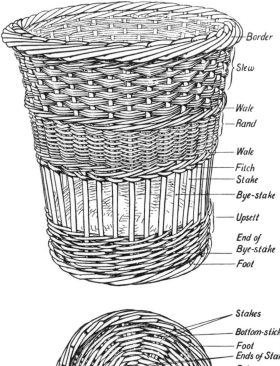

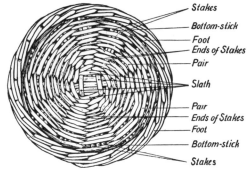

2. A diagram of an ordinary willow basket indicating the constructional parts and their technical names. (From An Introduction to the Art of Basket-Making by Thomas Okey)

The great renaissance of basketmaking by the Indians or the general public as either a useful or a fine art did not occur. For the Indians, the need to make baskets for utilitarian or aesthetic reasons was virtually gone. For them baskets had already lost most of their former symbolic meaning, their association with life patterns, with nature and religion. Baskets could not continue as an expression of a culture when the traditions had died. Yet the affectionate response of James and Mason to the culture of the American Indians, and the warm regard for them as human individuals, can not but be reassessed in the context of the present belated concern.

As for the general public, the lingering effect of the emphasis on basketmaking was the association of the craft with summer camps and merit badges, and with therapy in mental institutions. Finally, the word basketmaking was used to describe any non-intellectual manual performance, any sort of foolish busywork.

Thomas Okey's small book on willow basketry, published in England during the first decade of the century, illuminates by its matter-of-fact presentation, free of any sentimentality or preciousness, the distance we have traveled in jettisoning one of the most ancient and persistent handcrafts. The information he chooses to include makes his book ages removed from today's craft books with their basic steps enabling a novice to produce a quick and easy result.

Certainly since then the world has grown little richer in the kind of baskets which Mason, James, and the others revered. The degeneration in Indian basketmaking has not been checked. Indeed, many of the fine baskets which were extant when Mason and James were writing have by now been destroyed. The prevalence of old baskets even today suggests the awesome number which existed in the past, and their significance to earlier cultures.

Fortunately, baskets were appreciated by countless amateur collectors. While many such collected items have been acquired by museums, many more have been auctioned off in estate sales or sold to second-hand stores. Still others have been discarded. And although there is now a strong impulse to preserve these handmade objects which will never be made again, there is also a new willingness to "use" and enjoy such things, with emphasis on the "now," free of any heavy responsibility to preserve in a so-uncertain world.

Even when they are not used, but are only preserved, baskets are subject to destruction. They become brittle; they tear down from their rims, or the bottoms break apart from the side walls. Merely touching a brittle basket can cause it to split. I recently saw a wondrous group of Northwest Coast baskets. The colors are as fresh and the materials as lustrous as when the baskets were made. Yet all these Tlingit baskets, which show no sign of wear, with all their brand-newness of color and texture, are torn and broken because they were once poorly crated while being preserved.

Baskets have been called the most destructible of all textile constructions. Unlike ceramics, few very ancient baskets have managed to survive.

3. Tlingit twined basket, Northwest Coast, southern Alaska. Although the colors are unfaded and the materials seem brand-new, the basket is split down the side from being poorly packed and stored.

Yet through the persistence of tradition, through the extreme conservatism which has made basketry virtually changeless, baskets have withstood all the destructive forces to which they are so subject: moisture, heat, fire, mold, insects, wear. Although the life span of an individual basket is very short, another basket takes its place. Baskets have been replaced, over and over and over, unmodified, unimproved, unchanged. So, through the centuries, baskets have shown a remarkable endurance. In their perpetual freshness, they are startling survivals from the past, as truly as certain Egyptian tomb paintings and Peruvian textiles which miraculously kept their newness intact.

When neolithic man was grinding and polishing tools, and starting to domesticate animals and practice crude agriculture, he was also making and using baskets. The other technologies of early man changed, but basket-making and baskets remained basically the same and constantly useful. For us to identify with the lives of individuals in such neolithic societies is as difficult as to identify with the clumsy painted figures in a diorama in a natural history museum. Yet these early people made and used baskets not unlike those we continue to use. Archaeologists who found woven cloths in perfect condition in an Egyptian tomb are reported to have used them as nap-

4. Egyptian coil basket from Thebes (2050-2000 B.C.). Already in ancient Egypt such baskets for toilet objects were being replaced by wooden boxes serving the same purposes. (The Metropolitan Museum of Art, Museum Excavations, 1918-19. Rogers Fund, 1931)

kins at a meal. This connection with the past, which the archaeologists achieved through a bizarre gesture, seems to occur continually with the baskets which are made and used today. In basketry we must feel ourselves linked by a common everyday object to our remote antecedents. At a time when the habits, beliefs, and institutions inherited from the past are being destroyed by our technological society, baskets impose a recognition of our own moment as part of history and prehistory, as a continuation of all natural history. If by some magic baskets from prehistory appeared among baskets made today, they would go unnoticed and would be put to use. And in a sense, such baskets do appear and we do find them unremarkable but useful. Today's Egyptians are using the same baskets that the ancient Egyptians used. And just as surely we are using the same baskets that our distant forebears used.

Baskets have figured in all the changing contexts of everyday life through history—like monuments which have acquired a special dimension of meaning by remaining the same while the human scene changed around them. Yet the monuments speak differently of time than do baskets; the constancy of the monuments is actual, so that they have become eroded and stained. Although they have seemed eternal, they are being destroyed by

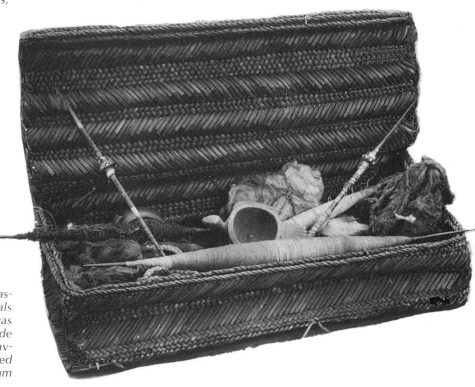

5. Peruvian work basket, pre-Columbian. Baskets survived along with weavings in burials on the Peruvian coast. This work basket was designed to rest firmly on the ground beside the weaver, and to hold the long, narrow weaving implements easily accessible yet protected by a cover. (Courtesy of the American Museum of Natural History)

the polluted air of modern times as effectively and as ruthlessly as great edifices of the past were dismantled by vandal builders for convenient building materials. And modern times will as surely destroy the previously so-destructible yet so-indestructible baskets.

Until recently, basketmakers at work were a familiar sight almost everywhere in the world. The materials they used were those that grew in their area. Everyone was acquainted with these materials as part of the local landscape. Willow, cane, palm, or grasses became baskets to satisfy specific needs and tastes. While baskets continue to be made from local materials according to traditional methods, the fabricated baskets are then transported to markets far away. The baskets still reflect the area where they were made, yet they no longer reflect the area where they are used. To the users in some faraway industrialized society, the baskets are as anonymous as their machine-made objects. If we take time to look at the baskets we use, we are surprised to discover that we don't know where they are from, what they are made of, how they are made. Although they were made to be sold to us, they do not necessarily express our taste or standards, which we can express in only a limited way through our selection. These baskets, made for sale, to be sold cheaply—the market considers baskets cheap and expendable—are made by the fastest methods from the most standardized and uniform materials. Identical baskets by the thousand are turned out by craftsmen in the areas surrounding Hong Kong and Taiwan. The results are as uniform and standardized and anonymous as machine products.

The hand production of utilitarian objects takes place only in areas where hand labor is cheap and available—that is, the underdeveloped countries and sections of countries. Baskets made in the United States are from Indian reservations and the depressed Appalachian area. European baskets are from Spain, Portugal, Italy, Poland, and Czechoslovakia. The cheapest and most plentiful baskets are from Korea, Taiwan, Pakistan, India, Ecuador, and Mexico. Baskets in our society are then associated with cheap labor and thereby with poverty, illiteracy, and the non-intellectual. Reactions to the occupation of basketmaking and what it represents have stigmatized the works themselves, old and new.

Baskets persist in our daily life although we know that they don't belong, that they are the antithesis of what our useful objects should be. They seem, if we think about them, to be bibelots alien to our society.

Baskets continually illuminate the gains and losses of technological progress, and the sharpness of the struggle between man and the machine. We know that baskets can be made only in underdeveloped areas where hand production is still feasible, and that the eagerly awaited industrial development, when it comes, must end the tradition of basketmaking. The sensuous delights of using baskets—of using something man-made that was used constantly from prehistoric times of hunting and gathering—will be lost to our successors. And basketmaking will, finally, change to become something else than it has always been. It will become an art, like hand-weaving today in our machine society, practiced by a few as individual expression.

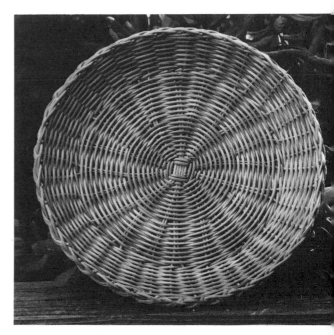

6. A simple wickerwork basket of rattan, from Hong Kong. Such trays, in various sizes, are made by the thousands, as uniform and anonymous as machine products.

7. Plastic packing material. This encasing, which was designed to protect fragile fruit during shipment, is like the basketry worked over gourds and glass bottles as protection.

Baskets, which have always been made by hand, are not being replaced by baskets made by machine; they are being replaced by other useful objects of plastic and paper which serve the same purpose. Mason's ancient plicated basket, which was threatened by the cheap patented ware made from veneering, is giving way before paper and plastic. Only for a brief time these replacements are imitating baskets until new forms are found and old forms are forgotten. Like flints, daggers, and polished celts, baskets will become specimens in museums, removed from ordinary direct experience and divested even of the limited meaning which they still possess today.

8. A plastic berry basket. The molded basket retains the look of diagonal plaiting, even to the vertical supports required by fragile plaited baskets.

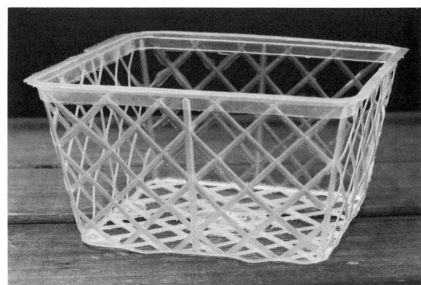

9. Bucket baskets of wood and plastic. Early in the century baskets from veneering were feared to be replacing traditional plicated baskets. Today the replacements are already being replaced by plastic baskets made in molds which faithfully reproduce even the staples.

While nothing is really new in baskets—a few bits of plastic incorporated here and there for color and shine and a semblance of modernity—yet because everything has changed around them, baskets are perceived differently. For us they *are* as we perceive them, in a sense they *are* different from what they ever were before. In the years following World War I the Bauhaus emerged in Germany with an experimental and analytical approach to design, investigating forms appropriate to functions, and materials appropriate to forms and, of course, design appropriate to machine production. Bauhaus precepts so influenced design thinking that it was possible, in the catalog of a recent exhibition, for the California Indian basket tradition to be described as based "on the concepts of form following function, truth to materials, and decoration related to form, all consistent with today's aesthetic values."

A few baskets have been changed simply by being set aside in museums as works of art. But most have been modified far more by their everyday participation as handmade objects in a technological world, and by changing values to which they have not been directly responsive. A more poignant isolation has been imposed by the twentieth-century environment than any museum could accomplish. What has concerned so many contemporary artists—the juxtaposing of familiar things in unexpected relationships to sharpen awareness and establish new identification of objects—has happened to baskets without the intervention or contrivance of an artist. The very sense of rapid change which characterizes this century has made baskets and their changelessness increasingly strange, less well-known, more truly incomprehensible.

The present study is not concerned with structural analysis and how-to-do-it. It is neither historical nor anthropological. It is a personal interpretation, concerned with the aesthetic quality of baskets as it relates to process and material and human impulses. What started as a book of photographs with brief descriptions became the occasion for developing a number of ideas about basketry and expressing my own insights into the basketry process in relation to other art processes. I suppose the real purpose of the work is to express my own love of baskets. Like Mason and James and the girls in their cubby in Deerfield, I must speak for the basketmakers.

1 THE OTHER BASKETS

In the Andaman Islands, between Thailand and India, the hunting-gathering way of life has continued into the twentieth century, apparently little changed from what it was thousands of years ago. An anthropologist, in writing about the Andaman Islands, referred to the baskets in the communal huts as the "real baskets." These correspond to baskets we are accustomed to see in museums and which we use in our own daily lives. They show careful construction and are treasured as part of the family's inheritance.

The other Andamanese baskets, those which by implication are unreal or less than true baskets, are common on the islands although they are quite unfamiliar to us. They are the baskets made spontaneously at a moment of need for a special purpose. They are used and discarded, as disposable as paper plates. For us the unreality of these baskets derives only partly from their unfamiliarity. It is as though we were asked to consider a newspaper folded roughly into a covering, or even a paper held over our heads during a sudden shower, as a real hat. Like such hats, these baskets exist only for moments during their short periods of use. The materials from which they are formed are modified so slightly, they become baskets so temporarily, that their existence as baskets is equivocal and ephemeral, and therefore unreal. Although their construction often conforms to definitions set down for basketry, we might be reluctant to take them seriously as baskets even if we could see them in use. Anthropologists have called them rough emergency baskets and temporary contrivances.

These baskets of the Andaman Islanders are made on hunting or gathering trips. They are hastily constructed on the spot from materials at hand, for carrying back whatever is found. Consequently they are of no standard size. They are specialized, custom-made to accommodate the load. They conform to the proportions of the person who will be doing the carrying—man, woman, or child.

While the thought is attractive that each basket is an individual constructional solution to a special problem as it arises, the truth is that these Andamanese baskets follow a general plan, and the plan is closely related to that of their permanent baskets. Reeds are arranged like spokes in a star position, their centers tied. The reeds are then bent upwards, forced into a basket shape, and held with a circle of split reed. The spaces between the spokes are then filled in with available materials, such as leaves or strips of flexible bark. Because no excess weight must be carried, only enough constructional elements are used to hold the load securely. Once camp is reached, the baskets are thrown away.

Reeds are tied together, bent upwards, and held with a circle of reed.

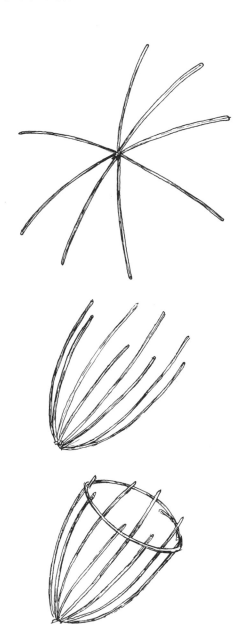

Similar baskets have been common in many parts of the world. Small baskets were made at a moment's notice when nuts and fruits were found and had to be transported, or when utensils were needed for eating and drinking. Indians traveling to and from their hunting grounds for extended periods of time left most of their permanent household articles in caches in the woods; then as need arose they made baskets and bowls which could be used and discarded. The nature of the baskets depended upon the materials at hand, the purposes, and the traditions. In the tropics, scoop-shaped baskets were quickly made from the leaf of a fan palm by bending the outside leaflets and interweaving them through the other leaflets, with the ends roughly tied. A plate was made by roughly sewing together two large leaves.

10. Wickerwork basket from North Andaman. The surface is daubed with red paint. Shells or turtle bones are strung from the rim to dangle as the basket is moved.

11. A "permanent" basket from Little Andaman. A wrapping technique holds the reed warps in a tense egg-shape; the wefts wrap around each warp in turn as they circle the basket. A fiber strap hangs from the rim.

12. A basket from Australia is a piece of natural fiber folded into shape and sewn together with a few rough stitches.

A platter-shaped basket was made from small pieces of coconut leaf cut off the tree and split down the midrib. The leaflets of the two pieces were plaited together and the ends drawn tight to create a slight concavity with the semblance of an edging or rim. The leaflets were left attached to the rib just as they grew on the tree. A water container was made from a folded leaf or a single piece of bark pinned together with one or two wooden pegs or spines. In Australia sometimes a piece of bark was pulled from a tree and merely crumpled together at opposite ends and so held by both hands to form a concave shape as a water container.

Changing a leaf into a basket is somewhat like Picasso's converting familiar objects into sculpture. By making the slightest alteration in a child's toy or a bicycle handlebar, or by turning it upside down or associating it unexpectedly with other objects, Picasso changes one thing into another even while it retains its original identity. He observes and often playfully points out similarities of form. The object becomes equivocal and shifting, two quite different things simultaneously.

13. Old Chinese traveling box for carrying toilet articles, Hangchow, Che-Kiang. Sheets of wood fiber are bent into the basket shape. Although the basket is the ultimate in refinement of craftsmanship and decoration, it recalls the crude Australian basket. (Field Museum of Natural History)

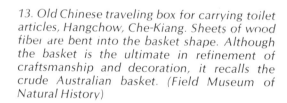

14. Rough basket from Northern Territory, Australia. The sheet of fiber is precisely folded so that the basket becomes rectangular.

15. Square picnic basket of plaiting and bamboo strips, from China, Ning-Po, Che-Kiang. Like the rough Australian basket, this picnic basket is forced into a neat rectangle. The bamboo strips are carved and painted black. The basket closes with a metal bar and padlock. The entire construction is a very permanent art object. (Field Museum of Natural History)

16. A basket for which no location is specified, although it is similar to other baskets from Australia.

17. Another view of the basket. The shape of the folded fiber is especially elegant and refined, in keeping with the configuration of the strip which holds the handle, and the decorative plaiting.

18. *Water-carrying vessel from Richmond River, N.E., New South Wales, Australia. The folding and binding create a strudy basket. (Courtesy of the American Museum of Natural History)*

A leaf-basket, which at the same time is both a leaf and a basket, may seem ingenious, just as the Picasso sculptures may appear clever, humorous, contrived. But more than that, it points up with a sort of joy, which is present also in the work of Picasso, the happy circumstance that a leaf can grow so like a basket, or that a basket is after all only a paraphrase of a leaf.

This simultaneous identification as man-made object and as natural form is denied to permanent baskets, even to those that consciously imitate the shape or growth pattern of a leaf.

19. Huckleberry basket, Warm Spring Interior, Pacific Northwest. A sheet of bark is shaped and sewn together, with a reinforcement which protects the fragile cut edge at the basket's rim.

20. Detail showing how the bark is sewn with a cord.

21. Birch-bark basket, Skeena River Indians, Hazelton, British Columbia. The peeled bark is cut to shape and sewn, with a reinforcement at the rim.

22. Birch-bark basket, Athabasca, Canada. The seam is elaborated with serrated strips of bark, which are used also as reinforcements at the rim and base. The rim is elaborately strengthened and is decorated with glass beads and leather fringe.

23. Birch-bark tub for koumiss, and birch-bark box for clothing, Yakut, Siberia. The stitchings and reinforcements are refined, and elaborated with decorations. (Courtesy of the American Museum of Natural History)

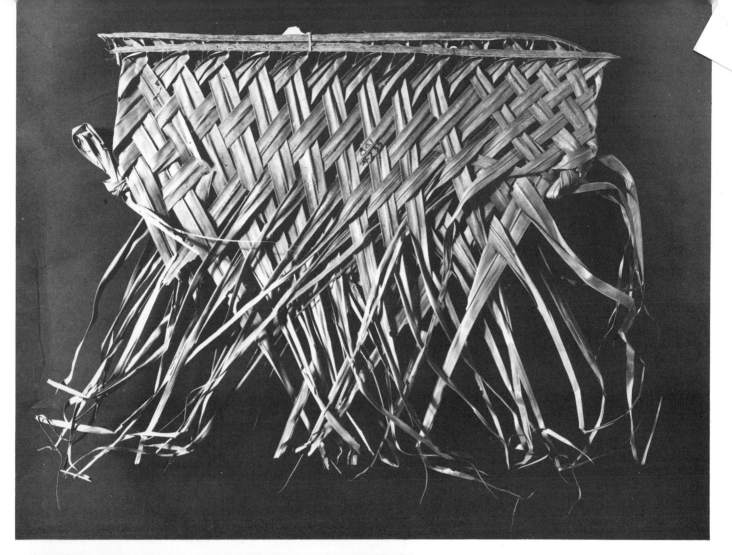

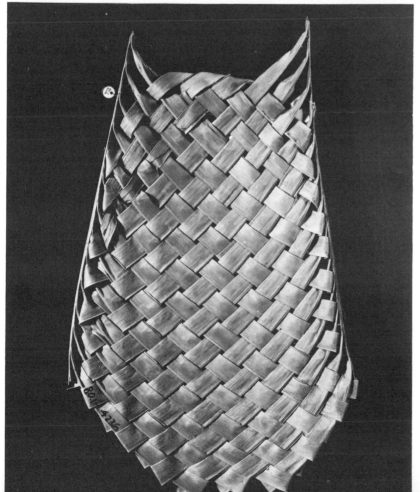

24. Plaited palm thatch sample for a roof, Mangaia, Cook Islands, South Pacific. This sample shows how the leaflets are perfectly arranged for plaiting. In the construction the leaflets lie flat and ribbon-like. (Courtesy of the American Museum of Natural History)

25. Plaited palm target used in Tupe game, Mangaia, Cook Islands, South Pacific. The split ribs are opposed and plaited, with the ends of the leaflets neatly folded and woven back into the construction. Such an article could just as well serve as a basket tray. (Courtesy of the American Museum of Natural History)

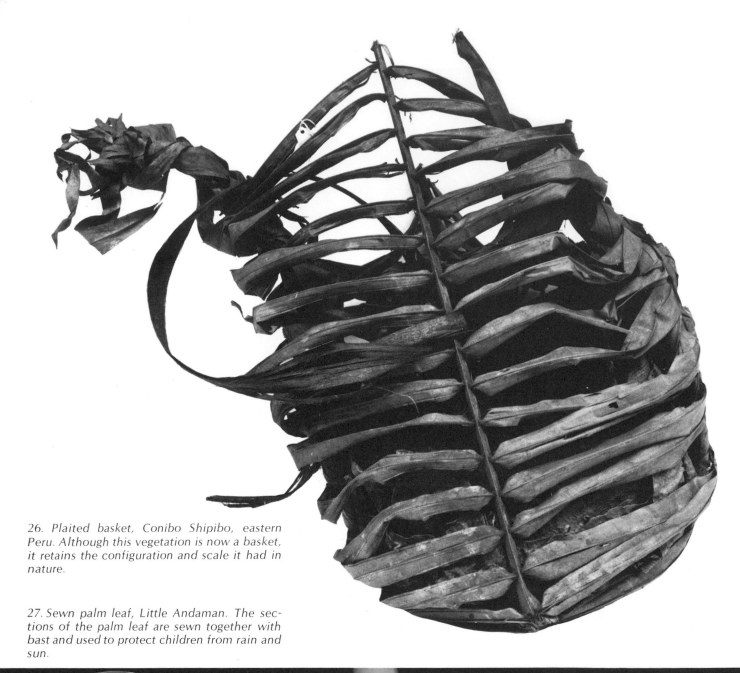

26. *Plaited basket, Conibo Shipibo, eastern Peru. Although this vegetation is now a basket, it retains the configuration and scale it had in nature.*

27. *Sewn palm leaf, Little Andaman. The sections of the palm leaf are sewn together with bast and used to protect children from rain and sun.*

The equivocal nature of temporary baskets recalls the ceremonial palms of Spain and Mexico for Palm Sunday. A length of palm leaf is cut off and the leaflets are plaited to turn a familiar leaf into a decorative object to be carried or to be hung on a balcony. These creations are sometimes less spontaneous and direct than the simple platter or scoop baskets using similar materials and techniques, for the fronds may be prepared in advance while still growing on the tree, by special wrapping to keep them from turning green. Consequently, even when just constructed, they lack the fresh color of the green palm, but instead show a paleness, artificial and achromatized.

28. *Plaited palm leaves from San Miguel de Allende, Mexico. These decorative palms are traditional in the Palm Sunday celebration of resurrection and renewal.*

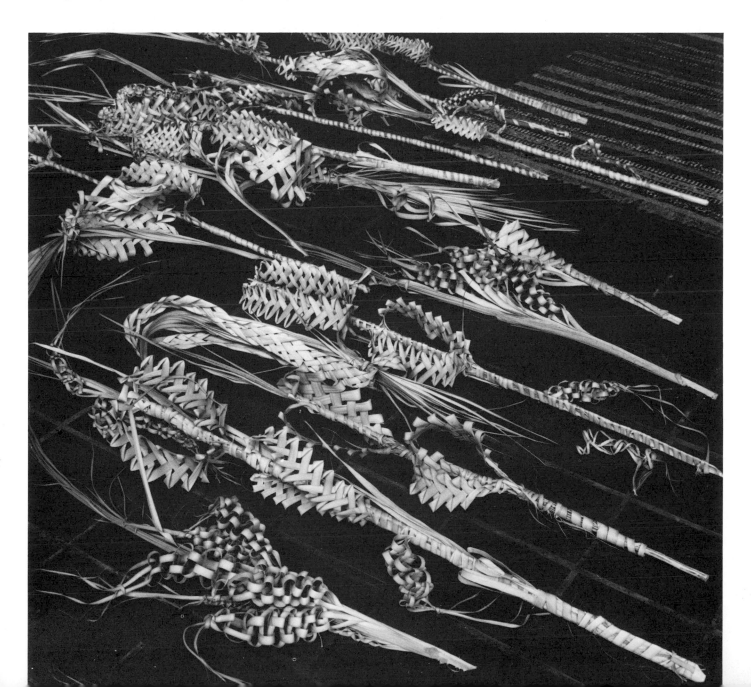

29. *Detail of a palm leaf from San Miguel de Allende, Mexico. Knots and straggly ends and split fiber strands are essential to the total decorative effect.*

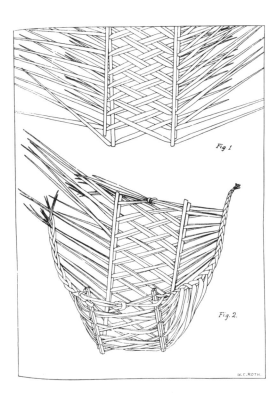

31. Diagram by W. E. Roth of a plaited palm basket. The drawing shows clearly the plaiting of the leaflets still attached to the ribs, and the braiding and knotting of the ends.

They seem pure, yet strangely wraithlike, appropriate to the awesome religious ceremony. The plaiting and interlacing are often complicated and refined to match the white fronds. The midrib sometimes remains dominant as in nature, yet elaborated with plaiting, while the outer shape of the leaf becomes pure fancy. Each frond is an individual variation on a theme. The familiar leaf is reshaped while retaining a sense of the original natural form.

The constructions and materials of some temporary baskets are carefully documented in words, and in diagrams such as those made by W.E. Roth in the early years of this century. The diagrams are sometimes rendered so sensitively, showing such concentration and such a drive toward accurate observation and communication of the facts, that the drawings themselves emerge as objects of considerable interest and beauty, yet without imparting the special quality of the baskets. Descriptions in the journals are often augmented by poorly reproduced photographs of specimens. Almost invariably the objects had become wizened and dried by the time of the photographing. They seem to have been included only to provide substantiating evidence rather than to indicate the essential nature of the baskets. All these devices—words, diagrams, photographs—are inadequate. Even the few specimens preserved in museums are the palest corpses of something fresh and lively that once existed. Museums have not yet learned to preserve such materials.

The art historian James Ackerman says that students and scholars have tended, because of geographical distances, to seek from works of art only the information that can be conveyed by photographs, and thereby they have avoided essential qualities found only in the original. A variation on this tendency occurs with baskets. The essential quality of temporary baskets, like the information that can not be conveyed in photographs of art objects, can not be directly communicated—either by the preservation of the object or by description of it. Therefore these baskets are misunderstood, or neglected and avoided in favor of other baskets.

32. Palm baskets from the Pomeroon District, as shown in the Journal of the Royal Anthropological Institute of Great Britain and Ireland, "Some Technical Notes from the Pomeroon District, British Guiana," Vol. XLI (1911).

Impossible as the task may seem short of our directly participating in a hunting-gathering society, we should experience temporary baskets not merely because of their abundance and significance throughout many thousands of years (although they have left scarcely a trace); and not only as research into something betokening the ancient antecedents of our common basket, providing insight into the *idea* of baskets and the nature of the basketry process; but most of all because temporary baskets possess unique aesthetic qualities to be enjoyed, no matter how indirectly. An appreciation of temporary baskets can enhance the response to all baskets.

Unfortunately, the temporary baskets which are photographed here can only faintly suggest what the baskets once were. While dried and disintegrating specimens may be adequate for scientific study of structure and identification of materials, they are like many of the ancient textile cloth fragments which have survived to provide invaluable information about textile history without ever imparting a sense of the original aesthetic quality of the textiles.

In looking at these photographs, the observer is required to perform a feat of reconstruction calling upon his sensory experiences, together with the associations evoked by such recalled stimuli. The imagined restoration of these baskets is a creative act based most of all on sensory responses to natural vegetation. The viewer responds not to the textures, odors, colors, sounds, and feel of the dried objects as they appear in the photographs, but to the objects as they were at the time of their construction. The photographs are a kind of notation which can, to the tuned-in observer, elicit the original object, just as the musical score can be transformed without an actual performance into sounds for the trained musician to respond to and evaluate; just as the blueprint can be read by an architect as a means of experiencing, to some degree at least, the architectural space.

Temporary baskets satisfy a romantic longing of man in an industrial society. They speak of a kind of self-sufficiency, a liberation from the common reliance on all the paraphernalia of contemporary life. Man can survive free, not weighted down with possessions, secure in his ability to manipulate grass, leaves, roots, and twigs to satisfy primary needs without reliance on any tools or machinery. The evidence presented here is able, only by implication, to reinforce the dream.

In handling temporary baskets preserved in museums, the most noticeable feature is the dryness—the appearance is dry; the tactile sensation, dry; the sound of the baskets as they move, dry. They lack the flexibility of some permanent baskets, and the firmness and rigidity combined with a subtle resilience, of others. What was once flexible has been immobilized in chance positions. Openings which dried flattened can not be reopened even to insert one's hand without breaking the crisp elements. The permanence achieved by these temporary baskets is useless; the single position, delicately maintained, is the only alternative to an absolute shattering.

Just as fresh temporary baskets show more than permanent baskets the life quality of the materials, so old temporary baskets which were somehow preserved show more than the permanent baskets the dead quality of the materials. These dried temporary baskets illuminate a quality of permanent baskets: after undergoing the processes of preparation, the materials of permanent baskets appear neither alive nor dead; the life quality of permanent baskets derives from something other than the life aspect of their materials.

The materials of temporary baskets, more than those of any other textile art, retain for their short lives the look that they have in nature. The reeds look like reeds, the leaves look like leaves, the bark looks like bark. The animal and vegetal fibers used in other textiles—in weaving, knitting, lace, etc.—are greatly modified to impart qualities of length, strength, color, or uniformity of dimension, which these materials do not have in their natural state. Probably silk of all the traditional textile fibers undergoes the least change in becoming yarn, yet even it had so lost its identity when it first appeared in textiles that its origin was a great mystery and stimulated wild speculation as to what it might be.

With the contemporary concern for a kind of purity in the use of materials, as a reaction against the anonymity and unfamiliarity of many man-made materials, a tendency is evident in many arts to declare the material's origin. Wool is incorporated in textiles virtually unspun, and is allowed to lie on the textile surface as though it had never been sheared. Simultaneously, a rough vigor is sought in reaction to the overly refined, genteel, and machine-like. The materials for temporary baskets always retained their identity, always showed their origin as living matter. The flexibility, fleshiness, and moist surface of the growing material, the life quality, were in the fresh basket for its moment. The plant and the basket shared the same life. The color, the odor, the feel of fresh-cut vegetation were part of the sensory experience of the basketmaking and the using of the basket, rather than being limited, as in permanent baskets, to the time of collecting and preparing the materials.

The structures of the dry baskets on the museum shelves are loose and separated. Elements have shrunk to a fraction of their original dimension, and instead of remaining flat have warped and buckled. Basket shapes have become completely distorted, like fallen leaves which curl into fantastic and unexpected forms, no two alike. In drying, the interwoven elements have withdrawn from each other as though repelled—so different from the tight structural involvement of elements in old permanent baskets. As the interweaving and tying disappear, the original configuration of the leaflets seems to return. The strong assertion of identity of materials continues even in the dried stage.

33. Detail of the Fiji pot carrier (Fig. 51). When fresh, the palm leaflets had a lively fullness and luster which have disappeared with the drying, leaving only a faint reminder of the basket's original vitality. The leaflets are dried so that joinings which were once tight are widely separated. Yet the bold scale of the natural fibers and a sense of the natural growth pattern remain.

When the baskets are moved, the elements rub against each other. This is the kind of friction of elements which is avoided in permanent baskets, for it destroys the baskets. And with the dryness comes a lightness of weight unexpected in baskets of such size. It is the lightness of desiccation. The baskets no longer fulfill the expectation of appropriate weight for an object of known size and material.

The baskets are surprisingly bold in scale, bolder than they appear in photographs. In looking at photographs we tend to reduce objects to the proportions with which we are familiar. We know only the basketry materials which have been reduced in size by splitting and shredding. In the temporary baskets the palm ribs and the individual leaflets are undiminished in size, and therefore they seem stridently off-size. Even the dried remains, because of the clearly retained identity of the original leaflets and ribs, suggest the trees, their vast size. They evoke, in a way denied to permanent baskets, thoughts of the wild landscape.

The baskets on the museum shelf still have an exuberance, a vigor and assurance. The authority of the basketmaker lingers in the dried leaves. The palm leaflets attached to the rib, in such a remarkably convenient growth pattern for basketry, some pulled forward, some backward to start the plaiting, still express vividly the controlling gestures of the basketmaker—a working with nature, using what it provides, observing and responding to the natural order and growth patterns. They also speak of masterly manipulation of great natural forms, of direct interaction of man and nature.

35. Plaited palm basket, Samoa. The leaflets are left attached to half the split rib, then alternate leaflets are pulled backward to be plaited.

37. *Plaited palm basket, Ponape, Micronesia. Sections of palm, each with four leaflets attached, are plaited together. The ends are braided and brought up the sides, on the outside of the basket, with the tips stuffed into the plaiting.*

38. *Plaited palm basket, New Hebrides. In this refined basket, the leaflets, still attached to the rib, are split and plaited in a twill pattern. At the base the plaiting becomes more compact, over-one, under-one, and the ending is neatly finished. (Courtesy of the American Museum of Natural History)*

39. *Detail of the plaited palm basket, Amahuaca tribe, Peru. Two palm ribs, with their leaflets attached, are crossed and tied together. The ribs and leaflets are bent into a basket shape, and the leaflets are plaited.*

40. *Detail of the plaited palm basket, Amahuaca tribe, Peru. The base of the basket, where the ribs cross, tends to be open. The ribs move up the sides of the basket, reinforcing the plaiting while providing securely attached leaflets evenly distributed for plaiting.*

41. *Plaited palm basket, Amahuaca tribe, Peru. The exterior of the basket shows over-one, under-one plaiting at the base, and twill plaiting toward the rim. The ends of the leaflets are braided—the braids lie on the outer surface and provide a reinforcement. Finally, the ends of the leaflets are bound together in the rim.*

42. *Plaited palm basket, Ponape, Micronesia. The palm leaflets are left free, to be held in plaiting only along the base of the basket. The plaiting is brought up as sides, and then carried through the rim to act as handles.*

43. *Plaited palm basket, Ponape, Micronesia. This basket is similar to that shown in Fig. 42, except that the leaflets move into the plaiting individually rather than as groups of three. This slight difference changes the scale of the basket.*

44. *Plaited palm basket, Rukuoro, Micronesia. The leaflets are attached to the rib at the basket's rim. After a short section of over-one, under-one plaiting, the leaflets are split into narrow ribbons and plaited in a twill pattern.*

45. *Detail of plaited palm basket, Rukuoro, Micronesia. The ends of the leaflets are plaited and braided across the bottom to form a flat base. The resulting bands vary greatly in scale, and show a succession of construction techniques, each appropriate to its special function.*

46. *Detail of plaited palm basket, Samoa (Fig. 35). The ends of the leaflets are braided inside the basket, providing the basket with a smooth outer surface.*

47. *Detail of plaited palm basket, Ponape, Micronesia. The flat leaflets are plaited into a flat membrane. The ends are simply tied. The knot and the irregular ends hanging free express the movements of the basketmaker.*

48. *Detail of a palm leaf from San Miguel de Allende, Mexico (Fig. 28). Sections of the fan palm are left unsplit, while other parts are split and braided and tied.*

Baskets which must be made in a hurry can use only simple and direct methods of construction. They never conceal, deny, or elaborate with extraneous material. Constructional devices which would not be practical in baskets to be used several times or for a variety of purposes are feasible. Ends of elements are tied off in knots rather than being concealed as though they didn't exist. Groups of ends are braided or knotted, sometimes left on the outside, sometimes poked into the inside. The constructional problems are evident in the finished work.

The direct manipulation of chance materials from the environment must have encouraged an improvisation and ingenuity prohibited by the rigid traditionalism of "real" baskets. It would be interesting to know how playfully or capriciously the Andamanese insert the wefts into their temporary baskets, and to what extent aesthetic judgments determine the selections from the available vegetation. With no concern for whether the materials will last or whether they will shrivel or change color in drying, selection might be on a different basis than in ordinary basketry, more adventurous and individual.

Yet often the methods, like the results, seem no more than pared-down versions of the more labored permanent baskets, or perhaps the permanent baskets seem like elaborations of the temporary baskets. Certain standards of craftsmanship seem as relevent to these short-lived efforts as to the more ambitious baskets. When the pinnate palm is plaited, the very regular distribution of the leaflets as they grow seems to establish an orderliness in the plaiting which carries through the work, free of errors which might not seem to matter. The procedures followed in these baskets were obviously familiar to the makers; the assurance is evident in the results; the act has about it an air of confidence. The temporary baskets may well have been, in their own way, as traditional and rigid as the permanent baskets. The direct use of materials is not to be mistaken for exerimentation with construction techniques or with development of new forms.

49. Plaited beer strainer, Nigeria. Although this very refined basket was obviously not made in a hurry, the ends of the finely split elements are simply bound and cut off.

The game basket from Peru is a temporary basket made from the rib of a palm leaf bent roughly into a square. The outer leaflets are brought up to form sides for the basket, while the inner leaflets form the bottom before they are brought up around a nest of leaves and bound at the top. A fiber strap is tied to the basket for carrying.

From the dried remains it is difficult to reconstruct the green palm, moist and cool, moving like a skin over the basket's contents, surrounding the game almost like a refreshing garnish. The basket was something to bring back, to open, to reveal the catch spread on green leaves. The luster of the fresh leaflets was not diminished by any interweaving or knotting. The vegetation was largely as it appeared in nature. The basket was an integral part of a specific hunting, bringing-back experience. This unity of basket and contents was most certainly felt by its users.

50. Game basket, Amahuaca tribe, Peru. The leaflets are still attached to the rib, which has been bent into a square. The leaflets are then brought up and around the basket's contents, with a fiber strap for carrying.

The game basket is not a self-sufficient unit into which things are put, but a wrapping which holds things together for carrying. It is not unlike a cloth with the corners brought up and around the contents. It seems akin to the leafy wrappings of many cooked foods. The basket with its leafy lining seems like a transitional step, half-way between a basket and a wrapped bundle.

Such bundle baskets can exist only in relation to something else; they supplement another form. Unlike most other baskets, these do not stand alone in any sense; they lose their specific identity apart from their contents. The shapes are largely determined by the shapes of the contents. The basketry is a close-fitting layer over extraneous objects, a kind of packaging.

This unity of baskets and extraneous objects exists also in more familiar permanent basketry, in the covering of Chianti bottles, coconut shells, gourds, and ceramic pots. These coverings could seldom be thought of as temporary. In fact, the basketry often imparts a permanence to something else that is fragile and would otherwise be temporary.

51. Fiji pot carrier. Split ribs are brought around the pot and plaited. The ends are braided and tied.

52. Wickerwork basketry cover for wine bottle, Portugal. The basketry is constructed over the bottle's surface to protect it during shipment.

53. Gourd partially covered with fiber, Mashonaland, Rhodesia. In a wrapping technique similar to that used in the Andaman Island basket (Fig. 11), fiber wefts encircle the gourd and adhere close to its surface. The fiber protects the gourd and provides a handle. (Courtesy of the American Museum of Natural History)

54. Coconut shell covered with fibrous cord, Micronesia. The cord provides a dense protective cover, a gripping surface, and a handle.

55. Twined basketry covering on glass bottle, Nootka, Washington State. Here, too, the basketry closely follows the bottle and becomes not a basket shape but a glass shape. The motif is described as a whaling scene.

56. *Melons with fiber tyings, as illustrated in* A Travers le Turkestan Russe, *by H. Krafft. This early photograph shows melons in a market. Each fragile fruit is equipped with a minimum fiber casing which ends in a loop for carrying.*

Simple tyings of fibers around fruits and vegetables to be transported—or around eggs in Japan—verge on becoming temporary baskets. Although they are rudimentary and sparse, yet the fiber tyings are functioning as baskets or basketry covers: the materials are manipulated in the knotting techniques of basketry. The fibers holding the clay pots for shipment in Peru just begin to suggest a basketry covering; the Mojave carrier, although it exists apart from contents, seems only the next step.

Occasionally we can discern the quest to inject into permanent baskets the qualities peculiar to temporary baskets, especially in works from Japan where basketry reached such a stage of refinement. Many of the Japanese baskets depart from the regular, the uniform, the symmetrical. These Japanese baskets use out-of-scale, rough, clearly identifiable materials. The baskets speak of the impossible physical strength and skill required to manipulate the most recalcitrant materials. Gnarled roots and great sections of bamboo with coarse nodes are interlaced with ropes of giant size. While these baskets seem to be coping manfully with the vagaries and eccentricities of natural forms, yet the irregularities are so carefully selected and presented, so self-consciously emphasized, often with glistening lacquer, that they finally appear (as undoubtedly they were intended to appear) artificial—another idiosyncratic contrivance in a very refined and ancient art. These baskets suggest a going beyond the temporary to the permanent, and then going beyond that to the permanent with the look of the temporary.

57. *Ceramic pots wrapped for shipment, Peru. The pots are roped together into a single unit.*

58. *Mojave carrier, southern California. Sticks are bent (like the reeds in the egg-shaped basket from the Andaman Islands, Fig. 11) and lashed to a hoop at the rim. The openings are filled in with cord. The weft cords encircle the carrier, wrapping around each individual stick and cord.*

59. Detail of Mojave carrier, southern California. Clumsy fiber bindings hold the sticks in place.

60. Bamboo tray, Japan. Here, too, rigid elements are lashed together, but with absolute
refinement and finish. The lashing is a uniform
strip of bamboo, which is plaited, wrapped,
and knotted, in a manner consistent with the
elegant bamboo slats. The whole tray is shown
in Fig. 204.

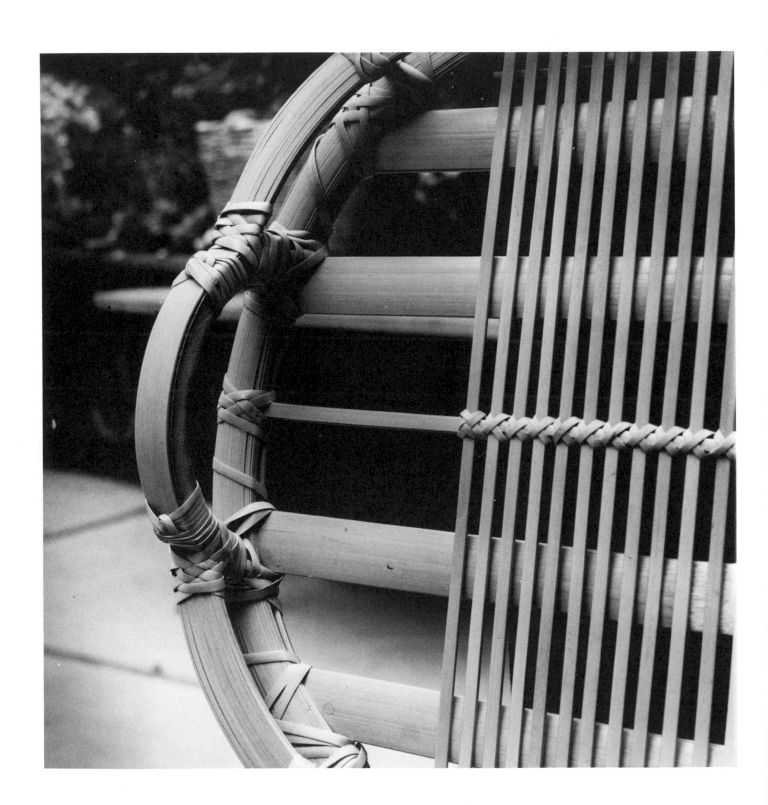

Although relatively few temporary baskets have been preserved—for they are as perishable as all the foliage of nature, like a cut flower put into a vase without water—evidence of their existence remains not only in such works as the refined "rough baskets" of the Japanese, and in practices which have been described by anthropologists studying hunting and gathering patterns. Also, modifications of such baskets have continued into radically changed cultures, even into twentieth-century Europe. Photographs show Italian peasants with extremely crude and simple carriers on their backs. The construction is only dense enough to keep the gathered materials from falling out, while the constructional branches are irregular, scarcely modified beyond being cut to approximate lengths. Although these Italian baskets were undoubtedly used many times, their rough appearance suggests a direct kinship with baskets made as required for individual loads. Photographs of the interiors of peasant houses show the walls decorated with many baskets; however, the rough carriers are not in evidence as treasured pieces of family inheritance. They can be easily imagined dumped in a shed along with the firewood which they so closely resemble.

The temporary object which by some chance has become permanent directly expresses only the nature of the temporary-object-become-permanent; it cannot help but be misunderstood because time has destroyed the qualities never meant to endure—the very qualities which were the essence. By their existence as preserved objects the temporary baskets have lost their quality of the temporary except by a kind of implication. They have a peculiar and unexpected force. They are like our society's expendable throwaways which should disappear fast, otherwise they become almost threatening. A paper plate tossed into the brush beside the road can seem to persist, to hang on doggedly to its existence, so much so that the same waste object blotting the landscape week after week and from one year to the next comes to suggest an instinct for survival, as though unless actively destroyed it would linger forever, stained and faded, as the last—and most significant—remnant of a civilization when all the monuments had vanished.

Temporary baskets in museums have that sense of persisting. They seem ancient and crumbling. And when they are handled, particles and shreds fall off, to be brushed away, a few fibers less. Yet they are like the wedding table in Dickens's *Great Expectations,* even the cake remaining over the many years, being eaten by the mice, but remaining. Somehow these preserved perishable baskets are like that cake, or the bread and nuts and lentils found in ancient Pompeii. The perishable thing which survives speaks most potently of time, of all time rather than the moment of its existence.

Built-in obsolescence is a familiar concept which we are coming to accept in what we consider to be our non-art utilitarian objects. We are trying to come to terms with the idea of a throwaway society. Today even architecture, which often has been considered to be among the most permanent creations of man, is being discussed in terms of buildings designed to disintegrate at a fixed and early date. Increasingly our art is not concerned with posterity. The validity of everything is in the "now." The idea of art that is evanescent or self-destructive becomes more and more intriguing. We enshrine for the moment the found object of no intrinsic value.

While we have come to accept the machine products of our own society as being expendable and, at the same time perhaps the most expressive aspects of our culture, we may still misunderstand similar profligacy with handmade objects. The handmade throwaways may be as central to other cultures as our machine products are to ours. It may seem incomprehensible to us that in a hand society as in a machine society the expressive qualities and aesthetic values may reside as much in what is thrown away as in what is carefully preserved. Our judgments of such societies have been based almost exclusively on the preservable, with all the limitations in concept and meaning which the preservable implies.

Quite understandably, permanent baskets have become museum specimens. The large Andamanese basket, while clearly similar to the temporary baskets described, must have seemed to the collector more important, of higher value, than the disposable product, and certainly more possible to bring back in a shipping case with its qualities intact. This large basket has a remarkable sense of order, and regularity of workmanship, as well as a substantial look—qualities we may tend to expect in a basket. It provides the kind of evidence of aesthetic and constructional attainment that can be appraised. And we may assume, limited as we are by our own cultural experiences, that because the people themselves cherished and preserved the permanent piece, it was more significant to them than the discarded one, as though saving were the measure of significance. Judgments have been made for us by those who are often uninformed in art—indeed by those individuals who often seem to possess the narrowest and most conservative tastes. They have elevated finish, overt craftsmanship, refinement, the genteel, neatness, and order, and the amount of time taken in the constructing as superior to, in fact as a sort of development of, the crude, vigorous, expressive. Vast areas of art are discredited.

With the broadened concept of what constitutes art, all preserved objects of the various cultures, and those described but not preserved, may gradually be looked at fresh. Storehouses may be opened to survey what was rejected by the scientists in relation to what was selected for publication and exhibition. The whole range of output may be reevaluated.

Perhaps the temporary baskets will then be valued and assessed. Those that are most temporary and least likely to be preserved in any form will continue to exist only as an idea. They are for a single use. They are associated with a single activity or experience. They are not constructed in advance during other times and in other situations. They cannot endure beyond that experience or occasion. They have no potential for standing alone, for becoming an "art object." In making no bid for permanence, in implying nothing beyond the moment's use, they are part of living nature—far more than the permanent baskets which deny, or attempt to surmount, the temporal essence of vegetal matter.

As baskets became constructed for permanence to be used from one gathering expedition to the next, and as they became made long in advance of their use, during seasons when time was not being devoted to other activities, they lost the sense of immediacy in their construction and materials. The rough vigor and the appealing off-handedness of the temporary baskets disappeared in favor of other qualities. Baskets built to last tend to require the use of materials which have been especially searched out, gathered and prepared. The time-consuming preparation, with all the handling required before the actual constructing, gives the craftsman a different feeling about his materials and how he works them. He requires something different of them, and of himself, than he does when the materials are picked and immediately manipulated into a basket. When the pressure of time is removed, and the urgency for a result, the processes can be different with different values in the process itself as well as in the product.

Given the choice, we may turn with certain relief from the permanent baskets to the unreal baskets which are so infused with life, with what may seem to be the essence of baskets. Who cannot respond to the joy of transforming some familiar vegetal material into a utilitarian container requiring no tools, no machines, only skillful manipulation of the hands? So direct, so spontaneous, so straightforward, these baskets suggest an innocent self-sufficiency, the simplest manipulation of valueless materials. In a few minutes they are again part of the natural vegetation—no disposal problems. In contemplating such works or in thinking about them we become aware that we are forever denied the experience of such products from another society; their value was in someone else's "now." But in such a simple recognition, at least our awareness of the human experience is somehow expanded.

PREPARED MATERIALS

Because the materials of basketry appear so natural, so like the everyday landscape, they suggest a random gathering of whatever was at hand. Yet because the various materials are so different in their usefulness, it has been speculated that Indians selected their dwelling places according to where good basket materials were plentiful. Although the Pomo Indians lived in the fertile coastal area of northern California, they used only a few of the numerous available plants. A long period of experimentation undoubtedly preceded the determinations, which were then rigidly adhered to without further experimentation.

Certain times of the year were considered best for gathering. Although the basketmaking itself could be performed during seasons when time was available, the gathering had to be done when the materials were ready. They were collected and stored for later use. Many prepared materials remain usable for years.

Basketry came to require thinking in terms of seasons and year, and preparing for the future. Some permanency of dwelling was required for drying materials over many days. They had to be straightened and spread out, then turned and lifted to expose all sides to the sun and air, and covered to protect them from the mold-inducing dampness. The drying process required time and favorable weather, quite apart from the time and favorable weather required for gathering, splitting, peeling, dyeing, etc.

The basketmaker tended to gather and prepare the materials which he himself would use. He had favorite places for finding materials with the precise qualities which he preferred. The gathering and preparing were actually the first steps in the basketmaking. Even Shounsai Shono, the Japanese basketmaker who has been designated a Living National Treasure, goes to the bamboo grove to select his materials. He then supervises their preparation. He feels that an intimate relationship with his materials is essential from start to finish.

In the preparing process, the materials change in appearance, not from their appearance in nature but from their appearance as live vegetation at the time they were gathered. Much of the visual quality of the natural landscape derives from dead twigs, branches, and seed pods left standing, and from old grasses, bleached and stained and disintegrating. The fresh colors and soft tactile qualities disappear, leaving dry tans and browns and the "natural" colors we associate with baskets.

Basketry which has any permanence is seldom able to show the colors and textures which belong to the life quality of a growing plant. Instead, the familiar baskets have a mellow, faded, last year's look. When baskets are colored with dye and paint, or lacquered, or imbricated with brilliant feathers, or decorated with shells and beads, the life quality of the plant material is not restored. Instead, another quality is imparted.

The Aleutian Islands at the turn of the last century provide an example of what was involved in collecting and preparing basket materials. These islands are known for their climate of fog, rain, snow, and violent wind. While the land is treeless, the vegetation is rich and varied. Hundreds of species of seed plants and ferns are known from this area. From this bounty the Aleuts chose the strand wheat or wild rye which grows profusely on all the islands. Although the Indians lived only on the coast and seldom visited the interior, and although the desired grass grew abundantly along the water's edge near the villages, the women did not gather the grasses close at hand but instead went inland where the grasses were stronger and tougher. Early in June before the grass headed, the women went into the hills to select their grasses. They gathered only two or three young blades from each stalk. The task was performed slowly and painstakingly. The selected materials were brought back to the villages and spread on the ground. They were watched and turned for about two weeks, away from any sunlight. When properly soft or wilted, the grasses were taken inside the houses and sorted into piles of coarse, medium, and fine. The coarse and medium-sized blades were split with the fingernails, which were allowed to grow long especially for this purpose. The sorted and split grasses were put into bundles, and for a month were hung out on foggy and cloudy days. During this part of the process the bundles were handled with a certain twisting motion to make the grasses pliable and tough. Finally the grasses were brought indoors to complete the drying process. At the time of the actual basketmaking, the grasses were further split as desired, sometimes as fine as threads.

After this long preparation the grasses ranged from straw color to almost white. For even whiter grasses, blades which had weathered in nature were sometimes gathered in November. They were weaker than the others, and were used only for certain striping. Some grasses were kept light green by placing them in deep shade for the first several weeks after they were gathered.

What is impressive, in addition to the care in selecting during the gathering, is the amount of sensitive handling over the many weeks and the constant attention to the changing conditions of the materials in relation to the weather. Nothing was chance or random; materials were not set aside and forgotten. Instead the chosen grasses were actively transformed by the Indians into useful construction materials. The basketmaking itself was done indoors during the winter months.

This preparation of materials, which is largely by-passed in making temporary baskets, may seem little more than waiting for natural materials to dry, to shrink and change color *before* they are used rather than after. Actually the preparation results in a certain subtle transformation of the materials which accounts for many of the qualities we associate with baskets. Materials which achieve a relative permanence through careful preparation can be manipulated differently, can perform in different construction techniques, can be treated as something which will be permanent, whatever that implies for the society involved.

Today, when materials and technologies move so easily across borders, it is difficult to comprehend a time when people of a small area used their own materials in their own ways, while adjoining groups used their materials in their ways, to satisfy essentially the same needs. Only occasionally were

61. Aleutian Island twined basket. The wild rye, split into fine, regular elements, creates a precise, flexible basket. The scalloped rim and the yarn decoration of small geometric motifs widely spaced over the surface are typical of Aleutian Island baskets.

basketry materials and techniques exchanged. For instance, the Chinook Indians on the Pacific Coast near the mouth of the Columbia River used dyed bear grass imported from up the river near the Cascade Mountains for ornamenting their twined baskets. In turn, the Quinaults, who were farther north on the Coast, traded with the Chinook for a raffia-like sea grass for net twine. But to a remarkable extent, Indian baskets reflected the plant life of the immediate area. Such parochial practices in basketry continue even today throughout the world where baskets are made.

While it would be quite feasible today to transport basketry materials, baskets continue to be made close to the source of the materials. Willow baskets are made where willows grow; straw and cornhusk baskets are made where these materials abound for other purposes; palm and bamboo baskets come from the areas which we associate with the growing plants. Even the coverings of the familiar Chianti flasks are made from the marshland plants which grow in the wine area of northern Italy.

In Persia, where mats of basketry are still used in the ceiling construction of the mud-roofed houses, the rushes are purchased in bundles rather than gathered by the matmaker. Presumably these raw materials could be transported anywhere. Yet the centers of the mat industry continue to be located near the places where the rushes grow in the river swamp, and the mats themselves are then transported.

A notable exception is the delicate Ischia baskets identified with the Naples area of Italy. The raffia used in their construction comes from Africa, primarily from the palms of Madagascar, so the basketmaking takes place at a very great distance from where the materials are grown. But this is exceptional. In considering the everyday baskets which are so common in our society from all parts of the world, it becomes apparent that the materials used indicate pretty well each basket's provenience.

In our technological society, quite separated as we are from direct contact with basketmaking, if we attempted to construct a basket we would probably buy reeds or raffia or rushes grown we know not where. We might assume that such a separation of the materials from their source is common in basketry, whereas in truth such a separation is exceptional today just as it was in the past.

To a very great extent the kinds of basket construction of an area are determined by the local vegetation. Places with similar plant life, even areas widely separated and without influence upon each other, tend to use remarkably similar techniques in their baskets. Palm, bamboo, willow, cane, grasses, roots—each seems to dictate how it will be used. And just as the materials determine the kind of construction, so the kind of construction influences the shapes of the baskets. Coiled baskets from widely separated areas of the world tend toward similar shapes, often with similar kinds of patterning and embellishment.

Each prepared material has its own special usefulness and its own limitations as well as its own prescribed way of being handled immediately before and during the actual basketmaking. Some materials are brittle and tend to break, while others shred and disintegrate from bending or they snap at the slightest pull. Dried materials have not the strength and flexibility of fresh materials. They regain these qualities when dampened, so that some are dipped in water just before being used. Others are soaked for hours, or overnight, or for days and weeks. Some are removed from the water and are wrapped up, wet, for more hours to attain the perfect condition for working. If they are worked too wet they swell with the moisture and become like fresh materials which dry out to form loose constructions. Even when damp, many materials remain incredibly fragile and must be handled with a firm sort of gentleness.

To avoid friction, trial-and-error, and the redoing which wear out these fragile elements, basketry techniques are performed with a kind of deliberation and decisiveness. From the worker's concentration upon the condition of the materials moving through his fingers, he may seem in a state of contemplation, almost in a trance. He appears to be in quiet communication with his materials. He is responding to their delicate nature, bending and folding them gently but firmly, almost molding them into the necessary configurations, and laying them in place. In the manipulation of willow and bamboo and some reeds, a rough vigor and strength of movement are evident—everything looks more vital and assured. But with the fragile grasses a different kind of control is exerted, which is what makes basketry processes seem so low-pressure and almost somnambulistic, so tedious even to watch.

Over many years the best ways for working the traditional materials have been determined. These are rigidly adhered to in an almost ritualistic series of steps. The know-how has been transmitted for many generations as invaluable technical information.

Like the materials used in virtually all textiles, most basketry materials are linear and flexible. Yet they differ significantly from those used in other textiles.

Each tiny individual vegetal and animal fiber used to form the yarns for knitting, weaving, lace-making, etc. has a linear flexibility in its natural state. Through the various processes of yarn construction—of combing, spinning, plying, and so on—these individual fibers are integrated to form yarns with flexibility, dimension, and strength quite unlike that of the individual fibers as they occur in nature as cocoons, cotton balls, or fleece. The making of yarn is a separate textile art. The various yarn constructions are constructions devised by man. As such, they have their own names, such as S-twist, Z-twist, plied, chenille, gimp, loop.

In basketry, also, flexible linear qualities exist in the materials in their natural state. These qualities are modified and enhanced, not through reforming or reintegrating the individual fibers as in yarn construction, but through the *preparation* of the materials. This is a reduction of the size of the fiber organizations which already exist in nature. It is accomplished by shredding, peeling, scraping, boiling, splitting. The materials are not reduced so far as to make them individual fibers to be reconstructed. The constructions which exist in nature are retained, but reduced in size.

The nature of preparation of basketry materials is clear in cane. Lengths

62. Raffia basket, Ischia, Italy. The raffia palm leaves from Madagascar are split into narrow elements which are long and tough. These are laced across the openings of wire frames which have been covered in a buttonhole stitch, concealing the wire completely.

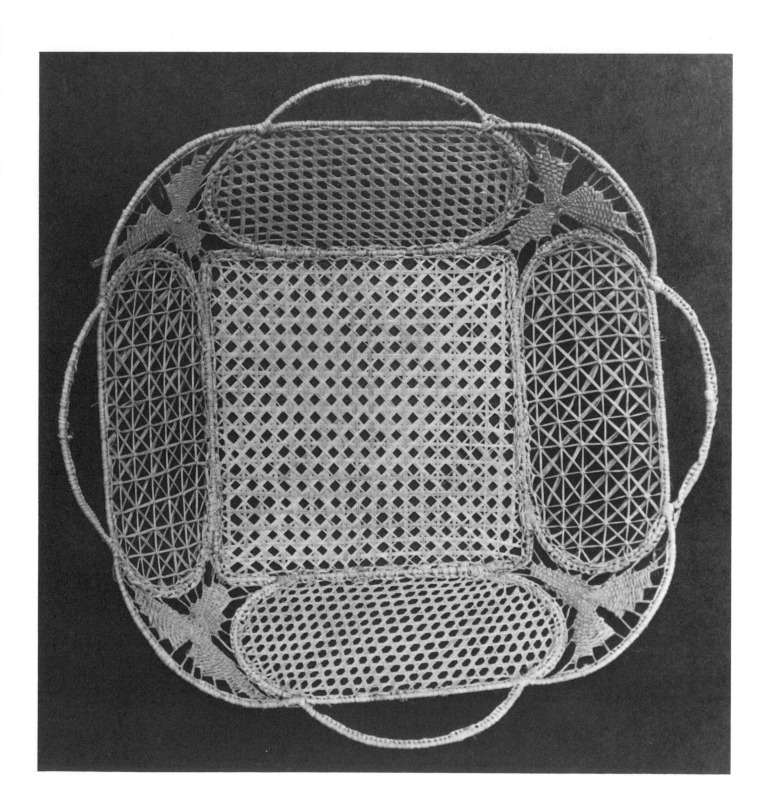

63. Cane mat, Peru. The cane which grows abundantly in Peru is smashed and flattened into strips for plaiting. The cane mats are used in constructing local dwellings.

of this round material are smashed roughly to transform it into flat elements to be plaited for mats or baskets. The smashed elements can be split into narrower strips to be manipulated in finer constructions.

The desired dimensions of basketry elements are achieved by subtraction, by reduction of the size of something already larger. Basketry elements are usually no longer than they occur in nature; they are seldom spun or knotted to increase the length. Some grasses of the precise color and texture desired may be only a few inches long. Others, such as those used by the Aleuts, are about two feet long. The strips of fanleaf palm used in South American basketry range from three to twelve feet in length. It is the relative shortness of the elements which makes possible their manipulation in basketry techniques.

While most basketry materials are short in relation to those used in other textile processes, very short elements are avoided except when they alone will provide a special color or texture desired in the decoration. Most basketry materials are kept the maximum length that they occur naturally, to avoid the constant running out and starting of new elements, which is time consuming, interrupts the rhythm of the basketmaking, interferes with the uniformity of the repeated units of construction, and weakens the structure.

64. Cane wickerwork basket, Peru. The everyday market baskets are constructed from the tough strips of cane with their glossy side to the outside. The baskets are unusually rigid and sturdy.

65. *Reeds for sale in the Nabeul market, Tunisia. These local reeds are neatly bundled for use in mats and baskets.*

66. *Basket constructed from woven reed matting, Tunisia. The woven mats, like the sheets of bark in the birch-bark baskets (Figs. 21, 22, 23) are cut into shapes to be bent and sewn together into baskets.*

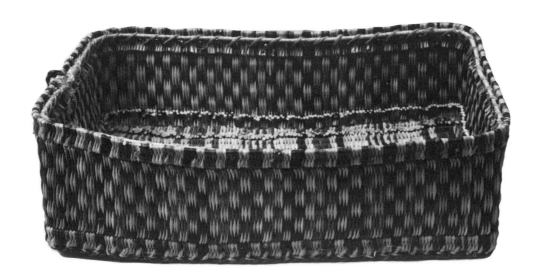

Basketry materials tend to be of a length and texture which induce constant tangling and catching on each other. Yet no help comes from the kind of devices which are essential in the other textile arts. Yarns for those other textiles are seldom allowed to lie or hang free in space. Instead they are stretched taut on a frame, or weighted, or wound onto bobbins and shuttles. In weaving, the loom keeps the warp yarns stretched taut and in order and holds the unused portion out of the way, while bobbins in shuttles carry the weft elements to be released only as required. In pillow lace and fancy plaiting, each individual yarn is held on a separate bobbin; the weight of the bobbin acts to hold the yarns tense and untangled.

In basketmaking no devices or implements keep the elements out of the way or hold them tense and in position. The reeds and grasses extend into the air or hang free, ready to catch onto each other or anything else within reach. Reeds and willows especially require a large space surrounding the basketmaker, for the longish elements whip through the air rather viciously.

67. Unfinished twined basket, Yurok, northern California. The stakes or warp elements radiate from the center. The basketmaker must manipulate the wefts through these extending warps without snapping them. All the loose ends of weft are left inside the basket until the construction is complete; then they are scraped off with a shell.

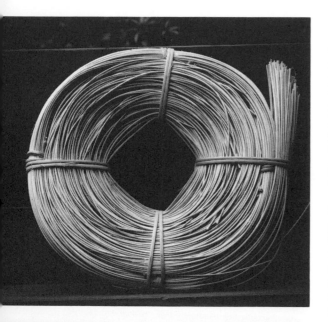

68. Coil of round reed prepared for sale. Actually this material, commonly called reed, is rattan. Such "reeds" are cut to very precise dimensions according to diameter, and neatly rolled.

Working with short lengths of fiber, unless they are treated as felting materials to be pressed or molded into shape, is possible only through an orderly disposing of them in readying them for the basketmaking itself. Even the gathering of a small number of grasses requires setting them in order, parallel, with the ends in position relative to each other. The Aleuts found it convenient to sort and arrange and finally to braid their fine grasses loosely to keep them in order until used. Raffia is commonly held in twisted and braided bundles which keep the separate elements roughly parallel. Reeds are sorted according to dimension and rolled and tied into hoop shapes. Willows are sorted according to length, with each length having its own particular name and use. The bundles of materials, like skeins of yarn, are as beautiful as the products constructed from them.

Basketry, like all the textile arts involving linear elements, seems to call for continuous and marked orderliness in the craftsman, and indeed to impose a sense of this orderliness on his product. The ordering, the arranging, the sensitive handling of the materials, promote a respectful response to the materials, their nature and beauty. The processes of preparation encourage a selectivity and quest for uniformity which shows in the baskets. And because the preparation makes possible more complex and controlled manipulation, such manipulation often tends quite naturally to be practiced. Prepared materials tend to induce a different sort of expression. Baskets become more refined, complex, uniform, controlled.

69. Raffia prepared for sale. The split elements are laid parallel, and tightly twisted. This tough material from the raffia palm is often sold to florists, as florists' raffia, for tying bundles of flowers, since it comes in convenient lengths and works well for binding and tying.

70. Basketry materials spread on a cane mat, Peru. The basketmaker surrounded herself with dyed and undyed materials, each separate strand held in a figure-eight.

71. Neck ring for winder dance, Bella Coola, Northwest Coast. The ribbons of cedar bark are twisted into a ropelike coil and bound. Strips are locked in the twist with the ends hanging loose. A minimum of manipulation of the elements allows them to retain their special beauty—their luster and shredded look. (Courtesy of the American Museum of Natural History)

3   BASKETS AS TEXTILES

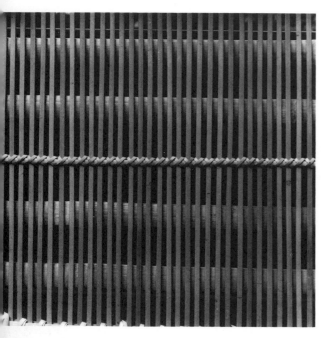

Evidence of the beginnings of the textile technologies perished long ago. Basketry and matmaking are generally believed to have preceded weaving. Coming later, out of basketry, weaving might mistakenly be thought of as the next step, a higher development.

Basketry and weaving are so closely interrelated that precise distinctions between them are difficult to make. The same constructions are used in both weaving and basketry. Basketry is commonly thought of as a process for producing baskets, while weaving is the process for producing cloth. The distinction is made according to the result. Yet basketry can produce more than baskets, while many of the objects we commonly call baskets are not the result of basketry at all. Similarly, weaving is concerned with more than cloth, and much that we call cloth is not the product of weaving.

Although the products of both basketry and weaving have continued to be useful and abundant throughout history, basketry has remained a hand process requiring only the simplest tools, while weaving has been mechanized, with more and more equipment constantly being developed. Weaving has been in the forefront of the technological advance. Changes in weaving processes figured prominently in the industrial revolution, in the development of the computer, and in methods of modern design by which specialists manipulate symbols and reference marks rather than the actual materials and tools of production.

72. Detail of bamboo tray, Japan (Fig. 204). The uniform slats of bamboo are not interlaced but are overlapped and lashed together.

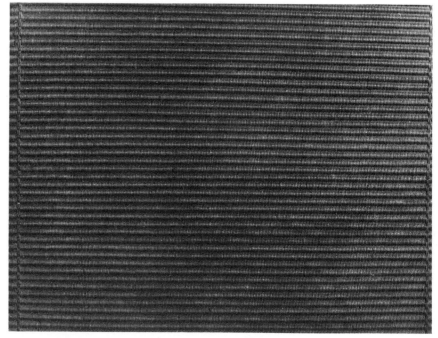

73. Detail of rectangular wickerwork basket, Japan, probably nineteenth century. The bamboo is split into very fine elements which are woven over uniform warps. At the edge of the photograph rows of twining are visible. These provide a subtle variation and define the rectangle.

74. North Andaman Island wickerwork baskets. The materials are carefully selected, including the isolated weft of yellow at the base of the basket in the foreground. Similar bits of yellow fiber, from the roasted skins of certain pods, are purposely worked into the nets and ropes from this area.

The fine, pliable, continuous materials of weaving—as opposed to the short, coarser materials of basketry—required the early development of ways to hold them in order without tangling, and ways to facilitate and speed the interlacing. Weaving and the loom became virtually synonymous, although the structures of weaving are possible, even from fine pliable materials, without a loom. The loom creates no structure that the hand cannot create without the loom.

It is generally agreed that a first step toward weaving was the use of continuous and flexible spun yarns instead of the short lengths and less flexible materials of basketry. This difference in materials relates directly to the differences between the basketry product and the woven product. The basket is a separate unit, while the piece of weaving can be continuous. The softness of the woven cloth contrasts with the assumed hardness of baskets.

75. Bamboo wickerwork basket, Japan, probably nineteenth century. The bamboo is split into extremely fine uniform elements which are worked with great precision. The braid of soft, pliable fiber which is tied over the cover is carefully related in scale and pattern to the hard basketry material.

76. Detail of bamboo wickerwork basket, Japan. The side supports are lashed with thin strips of bamboo. The lashings which move around the base and rim, as well as those up the side supports, all become refined and elegant decoration.

77. Detail of bamboo wickerwork basket, Japan. The bottom is flat strips of bamboo in twill plaiting. A heavy bamboo slat reinforces the base.

Thus baskets, often of so-called hard fibers, are known as hard textiles, although many baskets are soft and pliable and the softness is their essence as baskets.

Weaving creates what is often called a "textile plane" from two systems of linear elements intersecting at right angles. Basketry goes beyond into more complex systems and intersections. Fundamentally, weaving departs from the planar only after the weaving—through cutting and reassembling, through sewing, seaming, stuffing, gathering, pleating, folding, tucking, etc. Basketry becomes non-planar without seams or tucks, without cutting and assembling components.

A primary delight of basketry is in the way the vegetal fibers are made to adhere and assume configurations supporting each other without friction, in a thin, light textile membrane defining and moving like a skin over an airy volume which the basket itself has created. The elements retain their separate identities while interrelating to form something new with new form and new properties.

This supporting of elements is not, essentially, a sewing together as occurs in coil basketry, or a knotting together, or an adhering of them with adhesive material or nails or wire (although all these devices for holding are used in baskets). It is a disposition of the elements to hold them together, against each other, supporting each other, often under tension—one element pushing against another—all held in place through the positions of the others.

78. Twined basket, Tlingit, Northwest Coast. The basket is soft and pliable, able to be folded flat. The variation in the twining defines the basket's base.

79. Eskimo basket of plaited strips of kelp, sewn together, Pt. Barrow. An oval piece of fish skin is the center of the base.

80. Twined basket, Kamchadale, Siberia. The spaced twining creates a flexible basket, and clearly shows the color changes of the warp as warp stripes. At the rim, the twining is closer together, tending to obscure the warps. The result is a plaid. (Courtesy of the American Museum of Natural History)

This mutual supporting of elements to create the basket is quite different from another kind of supporting common in basketry. Often a number of separate linear elements are bundled together to form heavier, stronger, longer elements. Grasses, straws, twigs, etc. are laid parallel in bundles. These bundles can be of such monumental proportions that they are able to serve as timbers for reed houses and as planks for rafts and boats. Similar bundles, of smaller scale, are commonly used in coil baskets. The construction of the bundles is akin to the spinning of fibers into yarns and the plying of yarns into heavier yarns for weaving or knitting. But unlike such yarns, the bundles for basketmaking are usually not formed in a separate process, but are made as required during the basketmaking. The bundles do not exist self-sufficiently as yarn does, but are held together as bundles only by the stitching of the basketmaking.

81. Coil basket, Denmark. Elements are laid parallel in a bundle to create a coil of considerable bulk. The dimension of the coil increases as it moves from the center.

All the constructions of weaving—the gauzes, twills, brocades, double cloths, tapestries—all the ways that yarns are organized to support each other to create cloth and produce patterns, occur also in basketry. And in basketry these "weaves" create not only flat textile planes as in weaving, but they define spatial volumes. In a piece of weaving, twills move across from selvage to selvage and down the length of the cloth. In basketry the same twills move from side to side and from top to bottom, but they also continue uninterrupted across the bottom and up and around the sides. Often the form of the basket expands and diminishes, without interrupting the structural organization of the elements. The most ingenious accommodations have been devised to maintain a uniformity or a semblance of uniformity over the surface. The standards which the basketmakers imposed upon themselves, the ideas with which they struggled, can go quite uncomprehended by the casual observer. Solutions are presented so adroitly that the baskets seem easy, innocent, direct, obvious, simple, straightforward. The observer is unaware that a problem even existed, and reserves his wonder for the machine-like precision.

82. Twined basket, Pomo type, California. This basket is diagonal twining with light and dark elements that create a herringbone pattern like that in woven cloth.

83. Base of the twined basket, Pomo type, California. The herringbone pattern is devised to continue uninterrupted over the surface of the basket as it increases and diminishes in size.

84. Plaited palm basket, Ecuador. The over-two, under-two plaiting continues unbroken across the base and up the four sides.

4 WORK BASKETS

Baskets are often roughly divided into those made for decorative and ceremonial purposes, and those made for the workaday tasks of gathering, carrying, storing, cooking. Distinctions are never truly as clear as they seem in such a convenient classification.

The decorative-ceremonial baskets are the ones that our culture has tended to value more highly; they seem more like "art" objects and they are exhibited in museums. They often show great refinement of material and precision of workmanship. Obviously much time was devoted to their construction. To the people who made them they were often prestigious possessions, conspicuously indicating the amount of time for such endeavors free from considerations of mere survival. This expenditure of time is communicated to the most casual observer. Obviously too, the baskets go beyond the structural necessities, beyond any semblance of pure utilitarianism. They tend to have elaborate decorations, and often a kind of surface embellishment which is not part of the basic structure of the basket.

The non-structural embellishments are called *superstructural*. Sometimes they are strips of leather hanging free from the baskets, looking like the pure decorations that they are; at other times they form a surface pattern which appears deceptively structural. Sometimes they are not at all the linear fibrous elements one expects of basketry. They are beads or feathers or bits of bone or metal foil. Often the superstructural elements are dense enough to conceal the basket structure entirely, and the basket is referred to as a feather basket or a shell basket. At other times the superstructural elements are used more sparingly in relation to the structure. Even then, the superstructural elements are the attraction. They compel attention and seem to *be* the baskets. What is being admired and responded to is not the basketry at all.

85. Chinese carrying basket. This basket for sending presents of food combines finely split bamboo in wickerwork and twining with lacquered wood. (Field Museum of Natural History)

86. *Twined basket with buckskin fringe, Mescalero Apache, New Mexico. Strips of buckskin hang free from the rim, and at intervals down the wide leather strips along the sides. As the basket moves, the fringes are in constant motion, and the basket is seen through a veil of shifting leather strips.*

87. Coil basket, Assuan, Egypt. Strips of leather cover the coils and are held down at regular intervals by the binder. The surface of the basket becomes leather.

88. Coil basket, Upper Lake Pomo, California. Feathers and beads extend from the rim, while other feathers and beads are worked onto the basket's outer surface. The handle is made of shell beads.

89. African baskets, Ruanda, near Lake Victoria. The entire surface of the basket at the right is covered with beads arranged in patterns. (Courtesy of the American Museum of Natural History)

By contrast, in work baskets nothing conceals the structure, although some decorative elements may be present. The primary appeal is in the structural organization, without which there would be no basket. What is evident is how palm or rattan or bamboo or grass is manipulated to form a basket of the size and shape and rigidity and degree of openness or closedness required for a specific job. Satisfaction is in the taut structuralism, the logic of the organization.

91. Bamboo wickerwork basket, Taiwan. The complex arrangement of a variety of elements seems structurally essential to the sturdy basket. Everything seems in direct relation to the functional purposes.

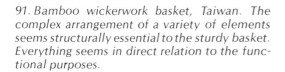

92. Wickerwork basket, Korea (see also Figs. 96 and 185). The cut ends of the elements are exposed on the exterior of the basket. Elements are laid side by side in flat, ribbon-like groups to make the center as flat as possible. As the circumference increases, the groups are separated. Similarly, the wefts at the center move together in bundles, and then become single elements.

93. Seed fan or beater, Wintoon, California. The twining groups the warps differently from row to row so that the warps are not allowed to move parellel but zigzag through the construction, making triangular openings.

94. Large twined granary basket, Cahuilla, California. Willow shoots, with their leaves still attached, are twined into this monumental mound of swirling twigs.

95. Detail of large twined granary basket, Cahuilla, California. The twined willow shoots move in heavy bundles. In the lower section, the dried leaves can be seen filling the openings.

Pleasure can be derived from observing how the vigorous, flowing curves, which some materials take naturally, are used for handles; how the smooth surface of materials is kept where it must be touched in using the basket; how fragile grasses of especially desired colors are placed sparingly as accents among sturdier materials; how elements are forced to radiate from a center without causing bulkiness and yet without leaving holes; how willow is placed so that its natural curve works with the curve of the basket; how elements strong enough to serve as a base are replaced by more fragile and pliable elements when the direction changes in forming the sides; how the weave and materials vary from one part of a basket to another for reasons sometimes structural, sometimes decorative.

A basket that swells and diminishes in a curve as flowing as the live grasses blown by the wind, or of a willow bending, or a cord whipping through the air is a marvel to behold. The challenge to the basketmaker is to retain the nature of the individual materials, which are such flexible lines in space with their own sort of fluidity, their own willingness to bend, their own kind of bend. Some are graceful and flowing; others are resistant, strong, and forced. There is the heavy movement of a coarse bundle of tules or grasses bound into a coil. And there is the stiff brittle curve of straw which moves like a series of short straight lines curving against its will.

When we look at work baskets we often have no idea what their specific purposes were. We do not know exactly what function was served by an openness at the rim or a narrow mouth or a curved base. Although these baskets are functional creations, we are unable to evaluate them according to their functional appropriateness. Just as the ceremonial-decorative baskets are, for us, quite divested of the full meaning which they had for the people who made and used them, the work baskets are devoid of real meaning regarding what would seem to us more obvious and comprehensible—their essential utility. We may know that a basket was used to gather clams, and that the openings in the basketry permitted the water to drip out. But that is a kind of "understanding" quite different from the understanding gained through actual use of the basket. Since most of us know virtually nothing about the nature of the materials or the basketry techniques, we cannot judge the appropriateness of the material or technique to the use. We cannot say whether the basket is a good design solution. While it may be true that—to paraphrase what has been said about woven textiles—the greatest delight offered by a basket, now as always, comes from the way one structural element supports another to create the basket, yet without a genuine comprehension of structure this delight must be absent. In looking at such baskets we see them just about as we see the ceremonial-decorative baskets. We decide whether the shapes, colors, and textures are appealing.

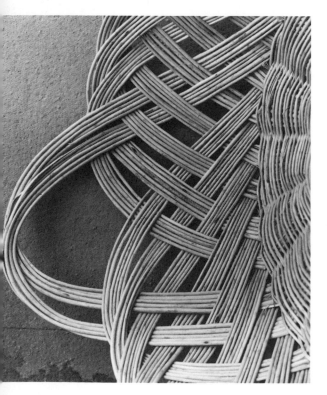

96. *Detail of wickerwork basket, Korea (see also Figs. 92 and 185). Certain elements of the plaited rim swing out of the construction in great flowing curves to act as handles.*

What we do is look at baskets, handle them, move them, and move around them, even smell them and listen to the sounds they make. We respond to their sensuous qualities. We enjoy the order or disorder, the regularity or irregularity, the apparent logic of the construction, the control of seemingly recalcitrant materials. We observe design motives, curves, and proportions. We judge even the most strictly utilitarian baskets according to aesthetic standards. Perhaps in insisting upon such considerations when appraising something presumably made only for use, we are closer than we know to the basketmaker.

The baskets which we ourselves use in our daily life were made for sale, usually not for specific utilitarian purposes. Shapes are standardized to satisfy a variety of needs. They are bowls, wastebaskets, clothes baskets, trays.

97. Detail of wickerwork basket, Philippine Islands. The ends of the split bamboo warps extend into the basket's opening, probably to keep fish from escaping.

98. Wickerwork basket, Philippine Islands. The basket takes an unusual shape, as eccentric as the fishing creel (Fig. 102), which for us is a familiar shape that does not seem eccentric.

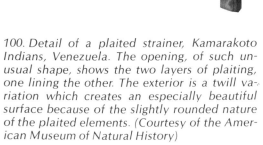

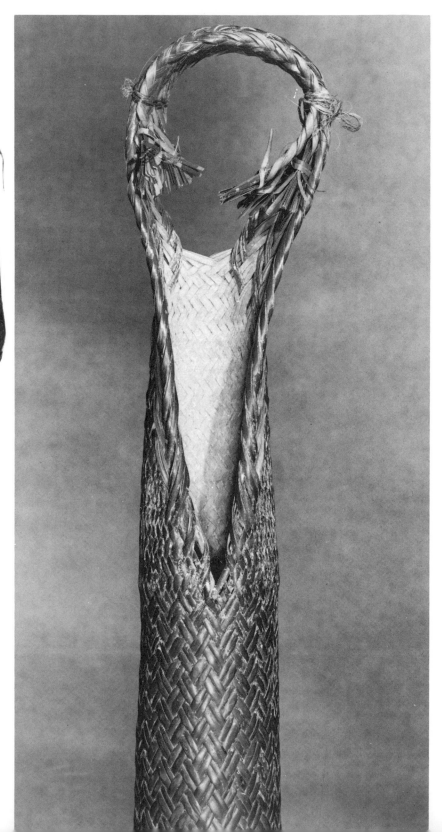

99. Plaited basket with frame, Kamarakoto Indians, Venezuela. This unusual object is a carrying basket with a bark carrying band. (Courtesy of the American Museum of Natural History)

100. Detail of a plaited strainer, Kamarakoto Indians, Venezuela. The opening, of such unusual shape, shows the two layers of plaiting, one lining the other. The exterior is a twill variation which creates an especially beautiful surface because of the slightly rounded nature of the plaited elements. (Courtesy of the American Museum of Natural History)

When we encounter in museums baskets made for very special uses, the shapes take us by surprise. The utilitarian basis of baskets is suddenly revealed. Great storage baskets set up on legs; milk baskets with lids as ingenious as those on our milk cartons; baskets with openings to allow fish in but not out. The shape often strikes us as eccentric, ingenious, contrived.

Because our direct experience with basketry is so limited, we may be disturbed to find it frequently used, unpretentiously and offhandedly, as required in conjunction with other materials and objects, so that it is made to encase gourds and ostrich eggs, and abalone shells, walking canes, and weapons. The shapes become those of gourds, eggs, bottles. The basketry is added to provide support for something fragile, or to make a gripping surface, or to hold separate components together, or to decorate.

101. Bamboo wickerwork storage baskets, Okinawa, Japan. These enormous globes are fishermen's storage baskets on the beach at Unten Village, Motobu, Okinawa. (Honolulu Academy of Arts Photograph)

102. Bamboo wickerwork fishing creel. The shape and the lid would seem most eccentric if they were not so familiar to us.

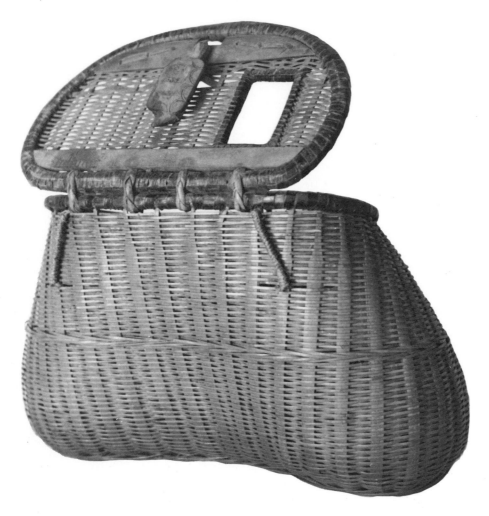

103. Twined dance basket, Lower Klamath River, probably Yurok. This ceremonial basket has leather ends and cloth-wrapped extensions terminating in leather strips.

Basketry also imitates shapes which we have come to consider appropriate to other mediums. Baskets have become goblets, compotes, teapots, and cups and saucers. We generally look upon such shapes as regrettable aberrations, a debasement of the art. Yet they can be viewed as playful and amusing, the kind of feat a craftsman occasionally enjoys performing. Artisans have long delighted in using their skill to imitate in one medium the appearance or shape which seems to belong to another medium. This sort of imitation occurs most frequently in materials such as clay which are known to be exceptionally plastic. In basketry such imitations proclaim the plasticity which could scarcely be inferred from watching the basketmaking process. If the imitations need to be justified beyond delight, they might be thought of as clarifying, through contrast, the nature of basic shapes we have come to regard as appropriate to basketry. Yet the unusual shapes of utilitarian baskets made to satisfy specific needs may seem to us about as unacceptable as the goblets and teapots, so contrary are they to the generalized, standardized baskets we use.

104. Twined basket in the shape of goblet (unidentified). The basketry stem cannot properly support the bowl. The object seems almost surrealistic.

1

3

4

Emphasis is on structural materials and their forceful manipulation. Variations in color and texture accentuate the various structural organizations.

1. Bamboo basket, Japan, late nineteenth century. 2. Bamboo basket, Japan. 3. Vender's bamboo basket, Japan, early twentieth century. 4. Construction detail of Plate 3.

2

The applied color of paint, embroidery, buttons, and shells functions in relation to exposed areas of brownish basketry.

5

6

7

5. Coil basket, Ethiopia, with horn stopper; leather straps decorated with buttons, and shells surrounding the base. 6. Detail of Plate 5. 7. Twined basket of cedar bark, Haida, British Columbia. 8. Twill plaited satchel, Melanesia. The basketry is embroidered and painted. 9. Detail of Plate 8.

8   9

5 PATTERNING

Some baskets have a showiness and ostentation, and often an exuberance, which seem foreign to the basketmaking technology. These are often gift baskets made for obvious show. The basketry structure is merely a vehicle for carrying the extraneous surface of pattern and texture. The facade concealing the structure sometimes adheres closely to the basket shape, while at other times it extends from the shape in fringes and other elaborations which camouflage the contour underneath.

The African basket becomes a massive mound of carefully arranged shells. Actually the basketry structure is physically incapable of supporting the decoration; when the lid is removed, everything tends to sag.

105. Coil basket, Ibo, Nigeria. Shells are sewed to the entire outer surface. Tassels are of red and green wool.

The Pomo basket is a marvelous reconstitution of a bird. The feathers arranged over the three-dimensional surface of the basket allow the light to fall in various ways to reveal the depth of color and iridescence of feathers covering a bird. Such an ingenious and painstaking transference of feathers, one by one, from the breast of the bird to the curved surface of a basket is a re-creation closely related to the covering of a basket surface with leather or paper to render the traditional basket shape in a material which is familiar in another shape. All the while, the basketry maintains its identity apart from the surface decoration. The basket is somewhere inside.

Some dense imbrication, such as that on the Klikitat coil basket, seems an integral part of the basket, so much so that the viewer may be surprised and disappointed to discover that the pattern does not carry into the interior of the basket. The imbrication, in this instance, consists of linear elements similar to the structural elements themselves.

107. Detail of coil basket, Cowlitz type, Washington State. The exterior of the basket is imbricated with bark ribbons. In some places the binder shows, but in others the imbrication conceals even the binder.

106. Coil basket, Pomo, California. The ends of the feathers are painstakingly worked into the basketry during the basketmaking.

108. Coil basket, Cowlitz type, Washington State. The imbricated pattern is like a skin worked in thin strips over the exterior surface. The interior shows none of the patterning.

10

11

14

Exterior surfaces are densely covered with vegetal materials to give these baskets their special character.

10. Coil basketry chest, British Columbia.   11. Detail of Plate 10.   12. Coil basket, Cowlitz type, Washington State. 13. Detail of Plate 12.   14. Nest basket of twigs and branches, France.

12

13

Colors, patterns, and textures derive from rags, yarns, beads, and feathers added to the baskets' surfaces.

15

16

17

18

15. Twined basket, Aleutian Islands, with patterns in colored wool. 16. Coiled palm basket, Tunisia, with wool yarn and rags held by the binder. 17. Twined basket, Yuki, Klamath type, northern California. The basket is covered with a beaded sheath attached to the basketry surface at the rim. 18. Coil basket, Pomo type, northern California, with feathers affixed during the basketmaking. The handle is shell beads. 19. Coil basket, Pomo type, northern California, with beads threaded on the binder during the basketmaking. 20. Detail of Plate 19.

19

20

109. *Twined basket, Panamint, Olancha, California. The pattern is painted on the surface, carefully following the structural elements. Such a typical basketry pattern could have been achieved structurally.*

When patterns are painted on the surface after the basket is constructed, the patterns often follow the structural elements, in configurations which could have been achieved through the basketry itself. The basket has to be closely examined to determine whether the patterns were painted or constructed. If the structure of a basket is horizontal-vertical, the patterning shows a clear horizontal and vertical movement; if the structure is diagonal, the patterns show clear diagonals. Significant exceptions are the patterns painted on basketry by Northwest Coast Indians. The same motifs are painted on the flat wooden surfaces of their houses and boxes as on their basketry. Similarly, patterns are often roughly daubed on New Guinea basketry, without apparent concern for the directions of the elements in the basketry—just as an artist in our society paints without following the weave of his canvas although it is an undeniable factor in the appearance of his paint.

110. *Coil basket, Nubia attribution. The pattern is created by changes in color in the binder, just as were the representational patterns of the Deerfield baskets (Fig. 1). The ending of the coil and the slight tipping are evident.*

111 Twined mats, Haida, Queen Charlotte Island, British Columbia. The closely twined mats of split spruce root show patterns through changes in the twining. On this constructed surface the motifs are painted, carefully related to the outer shapes of the mats but not to the twining. (Courtesy of the American Museum of Natural History)

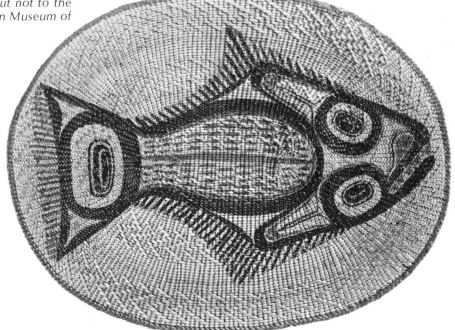

112. Coil basket, Ethiopia. This meal serving table tray basket shows lustrous colors of purple, red, green, yellow, and tan as binder for the coils. The rim and base are covered with tan leather, making this one of the most colorful of baskets.

113. Detail of coil basket, Ethiopia. Only occasionally, as the top of the leather strap, is the foundation material exposed. Otherwise it functions, like the warp in tapestry weaving, as a ridge over which the binder moves, creating highlights and shadows.

The basketry patterns grow from beginnings introduced early in the process. As the artisan works, the pattern materializes immutably along with the basket—although no such distinction between the pattern and the basket is truly valid. Patterns are built line by line, with no possibility of modifying anything once it is put down. It should not be surprising that patterns in basketry seldom look spontaneous or free. Months may be required to work a basket to its completion, and all during that time the pattern is developing from unmodifiable starts made so long before.

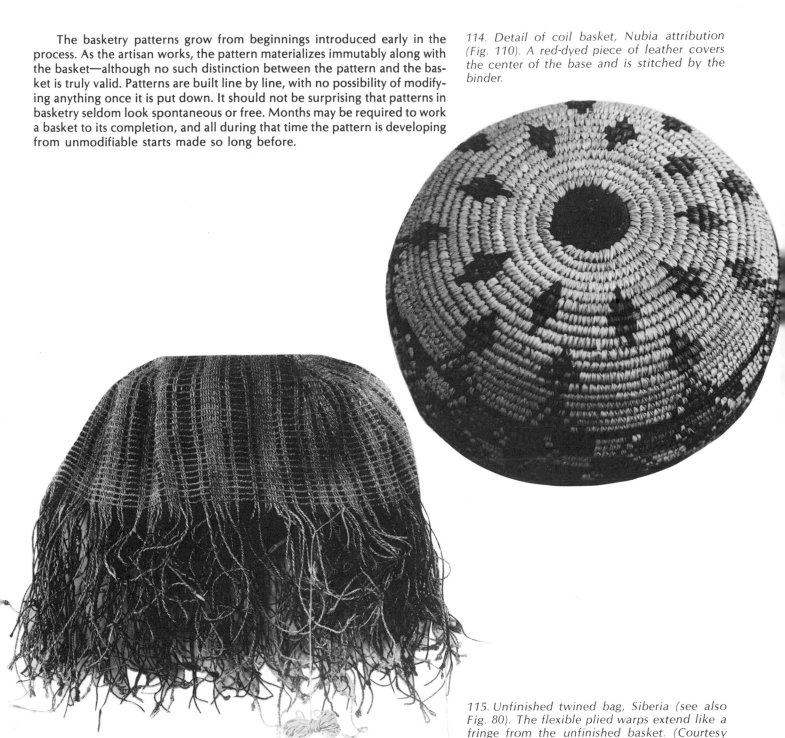

114. Detail of coil basket, Nubia attribution (Fig. 110). A red-dyed piece of leather covers the center of the base and is stitched by the binder.

115. Unfinished twined bag, Siberia (see also Fig. 80). The flexible plied warps extend like a fringe from the unfinished basket. (Courtesy of the American Museum of Natural History)

116. *Wickerwork plaque, Hopi type, Arizona. The kachina motif is worked from the center. The warps are large in scale in relation to the wefts, so that the modules from which the pattern is created are long and narrow. The motif seems stretched. The square in the center gradually develops into a square with rounded corners, and finally to the round plaque shape.*

Most baskets show the natural colors of dried materials. In other textile arts the fibers are often dyed, and frequently bleached before dyeing to make the color uniform and brilliant. With basketry many of the fibers would be weakened by bleaching. They tend to be used in their natural color, with a limited range of hues and values. The fibers used are often selected especially for their natural color. When dye is applied over the natural colors, the dyed colors tend to be dull and grayed. When brilliant color is achieved in basketry, it often seems at variance with the natural look of the materials, or with what has come to be regarded as the look of a basket. Brightly colored baskets, which appear in folk art, and in our society as Easter baskets, seem playful and amusing.

117. Plaited mat, Sarawak, Borneo. The pattern is created from structural variations in the plaiting within the limitation of very short floats. (Courtesy of the American Museum of Natural History)

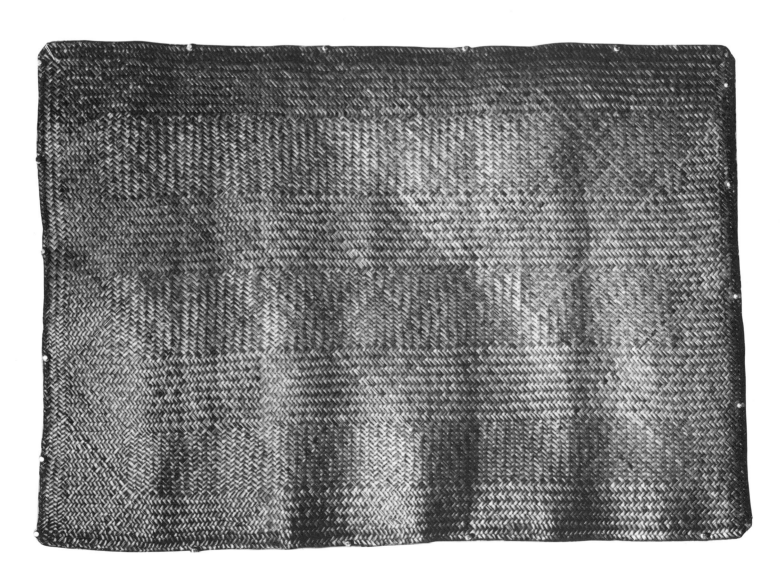

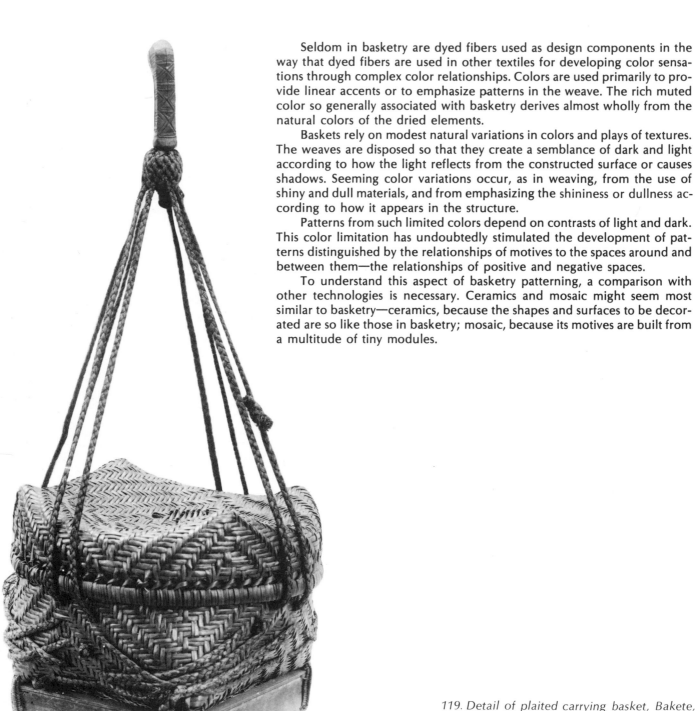

118. Plaited carrying basket, Bakete, Ndombe, Africa. The outer surface is enriched by the strands of interlaced braids which extend to the handle for carrying. (Courtesy of the American Museum of Natural History)

Seldom in basketry are dyed fibers used as design components in the way that dyed fibers are used in other textiles for developing color sensations through complex color relationships. Colors are used primarily to provide linear accents or to emphasize patterns in the weave. The rich muted color so generally associated with basketry derives almost wholly from the natural colors of the dried elements.

Baskets rely on modest natural variations in colors and plays of textures. The weaves are disposed so that they create a semblance of dark and light according to how the light reflects from the constructed surface or causes shadows. Seeming color variations occur, as in weaving, from the use of shiny and dull materials, and from emphasizing the shininess or dullness according to how it appears in the structure.

Patterns from such limited colors depend on contrasts of light and dark. This color limitation has undoubtedly stimulated the development of patterns distinguished by the relationships of motives to the spaces around and between them—the relationships of positive and negative spaces.

To understand this aspect of basketry patterning, a comparison with other technologies is necessary. Ceramics and mosaic might seem most similar to basketry—ceramics, because the shapes and surfaces to be decorated are so like those in basketry; mosaic, because its motives are built from a multitude of tiny modules.

119. Detail of plaited carrying basket, Bakete, Ndombe, Africa. The braided fibrous strands contrast with the hard plaited elements. (Courtesy of the American Museum of Natural History)

120. Twined basket, Pomo, Ft. Bragg, California. In the wide, swirling band, the pattern, in about equal amounts of brown and white, shifts from a light zigzag on a brown background, to brown triangles reaching into a white field.

121. Twined basket, Modok, Klamath Lake, Oregon. The pattern is completed as the basketry increases, with the motifs and background created simultaneously.

A potter has a bowl before him. He looks at it and applies his glazes or slips to the existing surface. He paints patterns in relation to shapes already established. He can start anywhere on the surface, adding motives here and there until the distribution is satisfying. In basketry no surface exists to be decorated; the surface and the decoration are fabricated simultaneously. Both are built "in the air." The patterns in basketry are envisaged in relation not to circumscribed spaces but to all the openness existing at the constructional edge of the unfinished basket.

Patterning in ceramics differs in another basic way. Both basketmaking and the ceramic process are series of steps. In ceramics each step is finished completely before another is commenced. An unfinished pot may have gone through the steps of forming, slip painting, bisque firing, and be ready for glazing and refiring. But in basketry, the entire series of steps is performed at each point along the way. So that while a half-finished pot is an entire pot that has gone through half of the necessary steps, an unfinished basket is only half a basket, but that half is completely finished. A potter working at a pot over days or weeks finishes a step, and next time is ready to start another step. But a basketmaker must each day perform *all* the various steps, uniformly and consistently, to conform to the same steps performed a day or week or month before. Like all the other steps in basketmaking, the patterning cannot be accomplished in a concentrated period of time but must be done continually throughout the long process.

In mosaic, patterns are made by arranging tiny components on an existing surface. Like ceramic patterns, the motives are established in relation to already existing spaces. But then, in mosaic, the background is filled in around the motives. Frequently the filled-in background of tesserae repeats and amplifies the contours of the already established motives. In basketry, no surface exists to be decorated, no background is to be filled in later.

The unique subtlety of the interplay of positive and negative spaces in baskets must be at least partly attributable to this simultaneous development of positive and negative. Both are created in exactly the same way, so that they tend to become balanced and, in a sense, to become the same. In looking at them, the viewer can be uncertain which is positive and which is negative. At first a light motive seems to have a dark background, but then a shift occurs so that a dark motive seems to be on a light background. Such shifting patterns are delightful and visually stimulating. They invite a kind of contemplation appropriate to an object of a size and weight and texture to be held in one's hands.

Dark and light areas can fluctuate as background and foreground.

In mosaic the tesserae can move out of the strict horizontal-vertical position to create, and reinforce, curves.

Basketry permits neither corrections nor adjustments short of reversal. Unweaving is extremely tedious and tends to weaken and wear out the fibers. Shapes and patterns become cautious, seldom innovative. The geometric patterns which result so naturally from the process seem also to be favored because of their safeness, their predictability.

The caution might be accounted for by the extreme conservatism and traditionalism which characterize the agricultural or domestic life of which basketry has long been such a part. Or it might be accounted for by the aversion to new methods and new ideas which is said to have characterized all artisans, especially those of early times. Yet it must also have been fostered by the very nature of the basketmaking process.

How different is the ceramic process. Clay encourages instant modification and revision. Changes occur quickly, effortlessly. The whole development of a pot seems a constant presentation to the potter of the various possibilities from which he must only choose. The shape is one thing, and in a moment it is something else, and in another moment it can be different still. The potential for patterning in ceramics seems as boundless as the potential for shaping. The potter selects from the possibilities presented before him.

122. Coil basket, Pima, Arizona. The pattern can seem to shift from a dark pattern on a light basket, to a light pattern on a dark basket.

Basketry is like knitting—the craftsman approaches, executes, and completes a modular unit, which is than forever finished.

Almost all textiles, whether hard or soft, are composed of repeated modular units or repeated sequences of units. In much plaited basketry and wickerwork, the elements intersect at right angles in an over-one, under-one interweaving. The result is an appearance of rectangular units in precise arrangement; the surface seems a sort of mosaic. Twined basketry shows a similar surface of units which appear as rectangles or parallelograms compactly arranged, and often alternating in color. In coil basketry, a stitch over a coil establishes rectangles related in size to the width of the coil and the width of the binding element. From such tiny units as these, textiles are built, and through the arrangement of the colors and textures of the separate units, endless patterns are created.

The patterns of baskets are obvious and direct, retaining the appearance not only of the fibers, but of the modules. Baskets are most often seen close up, held in the hands or at close range in the household. The distance from which textiles are viewed has much to do with whether they seem to be compositions of modular units. Herbert Read believed that a good textile is frankly fibrous in appearance, and makes no attempt to disguise warp and weft, even in the production of ornament. Because of the relative coarseness of their materials, baskets tend to declare their structural basis. The construction of the patterning is not disguised.

The individual elements of basketry never lose their separate identity, never merge or become transformed. The process, with all these individual elements, becomes one of regularity, orderliness, and repetition. Even when patterns are not counted and set up by numbers, they inevitably develop and are controlled by the module of the width of the individual element. For this reason basketry has a modular look, of an identical form or stitch of certain size and configuration, repeated again and again.

Basketmaking, as a series of steps repeated over and over, is an appropriate medium for repeated pattern motives. Such motives are satisfying to the maker for they provide variety in the doing without being too demanding. In a process so slow, even the simplest color change to make a band adds to the joy in the process. Some patterns seem to have been introduced more for the basketmaker than for any final visual effect. Bands and stripes and regular repeats can be easily worked on over a long time, even when the work is done in community and social situations, and when it must be constantly laid aside for more pressing duties.

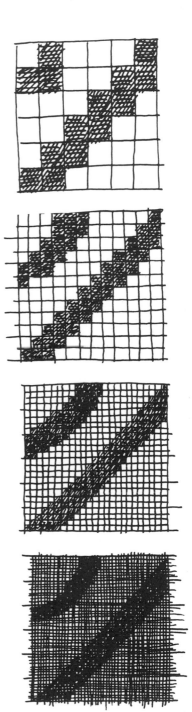

As the modular units become smaller, curves can become smoother, with less of a stair-stepped appearance. Finally the sense of individual modules almost disappears.

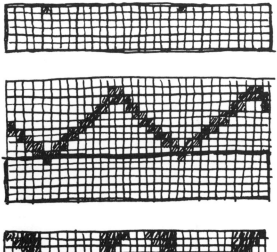

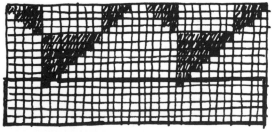

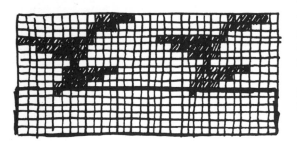

A number of points established at regular intervals around the basket early in the basketmaking provide a secure base for motives to develop without further calculation. Basketry is often thought of as numerical, with patterns resulting from much counting. Actually the process is performed pretty much without counting, once the intervals are established. As new stitches are added, row upon row, they take their places in relation to those already established. The process is simply a matter of moving systematically one stitch to the right of the pattern in the preceding row, or two stitches to the left, or whatever is decided upon. The most complex appearing patterns arise from variations so small that no counting is necessary. The stitches as they accumulate create a horizontal-vertical grid. The basketmaker's eye can move up the vertical lines of this grid for accurate placement of additional motives in relation to those already worked. Patterns grow by systematic accretion, by a regular addition to what is already there.

Some basketry is characterized by complex interlocking motives developed almost like puzzles. Obviously the pleasure was in the disciplined accomplishment of working such an interrelationship of shapes built up only from the bottom, nothing added later, nothing changed. It is a bit like working a crossword puzzle with a fountain pen. The challenge is in the immutable nature of the medium. These baskets express a wholehearted embracing of the medium with all its limitations—a virtuosity, a sort of performance, an intellectual exercise. And indeed as an art basketry must often be described as dry, intellectual, geometric, devoid of emotion, pure; classic as opposed to romantic.

Developing patterns by accretion is closely related to the method of developing the entire basket from the start at the center of the base. There, too, additions are made, in orderly, systematic fashion, to what has already been established. The result is numerical, but not a matter of counting. The artisan laughs and talks and is concerned with extraneous events while his fingers create the construction which seems to be all counting.

The ideas, plans, and calculations are in the mind of the basketmaker, and are "figured out" finally through systematically manipulating the materials in the actual basketmaking.

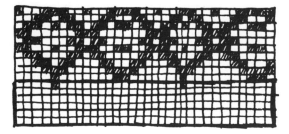

From points established in the basketry, as in the top sketch, innumerable patterns can be developed, working upward from these established points.

In an art such as basketry or weaving or mosaic, in which the structure is an infinite number of repeated modules, geometric motives seem to occur naturally in any patterning, along with a flatness of color shapes, as opposed to color gradations within shapes. Curves and lines which move freely are accomplished almost *against* the medium. When the artisan works directly with the material without any sketch, the structural directions seem to control the patterns in a geometric blockiness. A sketch made in another medium enables the artisan to overcome this powerful force. In tapestry a cartoon is painted or drawn, and this is marked on the warps, or the sketch is placed under the warps. Any curve or modulation of color—the fluid line or the blended or shaded colors which occur so naturally in paint, can be transcribed in tapestry. Indeed, paintings are frequently rendered in tapestry. The resulting shapes and color changes would never have occurred had the artisan been working directly on the loom without a sketch.

123. Chinese bamboo basket, plaiting and wickerwork, Ning-Po, Che-Kiang. The patterns on the cover and bottom of the basket were undoubtedly first developed through drawing or painting, and adapted to weaving and basketry. The central motifs are similar to Chinese brocaded patterns, while the border surrounding the bottom pattern clearly evolved from basketry. (Field Museum of Natural History)

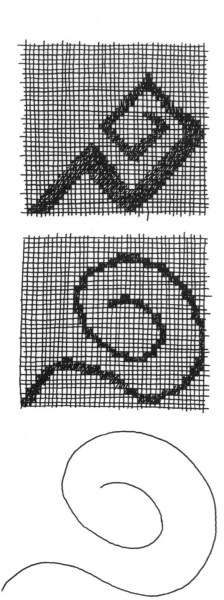

The top motif, figured out directly on graph paper, is very angular, while the next motif, transcribed onto graph paper from a freely drawn curve, is more fluid.

In some other kinds of weavings motives are often worked out on squared paper. They emerge as blocky and geometric, like so much peasant embroidery. But if a sketch is made first apart from the squared paper, and then this is transcribed onto squared paper, the shapes become different, more irregular, less predictable, livelier. In mosaic, a rough line sketch is often drawn onto the surface on which the tesserae will be set. Then the tesserae are laid along these lines. Often a line of the positive color is laid alongside the sketched line, and a line of the background is laid along the other side of the sketched line. Then everything on both sides is filled in.

In a sense, working from a sketch in another medium imposes on one medium what is natural to another. Since basketry uses no sketches in other mediums, it has remained peculiarly pure. At the same time, its patterning has seldom been enriched by the borrowings from other mediums.

While it is probably true that basketry is a continually creative process in that the design must be "worked out" as the basket develops rather than being precisely figured out in advance and then rendered, yet the "working out" has tended, from the evidence of baskets everywhere, not to encourage free, creative experimentation. Most baskets have the look of something done before, rather than something which evolved spontaneously through the actual working with the materials.

The "working out" of the ideas is largely a series of small decisions, such as whether to add another dark stitch before commencing the light stitches. Now, such decisions may seem trifles; observing them being made gives no sensation of witnessing a creative act. Yet they are of the utmost consequence in determining the aesthetic quality of the basket. The flowing line of the basket's contour results from a series of the smallest decisions, the slightest modifications of tension or pressure. The silhouette of the motive, the positive-negative spaces, the relationship of pattern to contour derive from just such decisions.

A line is drawn in the ground, the tesserae are laid along the line, and the surrounding areas are filled in.

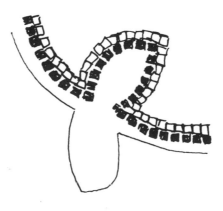

The two Pima coil baskets are similar in shape and patterning, and like so much basketry, tan and brown. The surfaces seem to be mosaics of stitches, with each stitch large enough to be perceived individually, to be counted. The baskets impose on the observer an awareness of counting.

The horizontals and verticals in both baskets are precise and assured. The diagonals in the taller basket spring from the base with great authority and certainty, but those in the flatter basket waver slightly and the widths fluctuate. Everything about the taller basket seems controlled, cool, and precisely calculated—tense, compact, energetic, perhaps mechanical. The intervals of dark and light where the pattern commences toward the base were accurately calculated for the development of the motives. By contrast, the pattern of the flatter basket seems a little relaxed and sprawling. The calculations were less accurate, so that obvious adjustments had to be made to accommodate the motives as they developed.

The flatter basket is decorated with beads around the rim, softening the appearance of the top edge. The taller basket ends severely, consistent with its measured look, its sense of being a sharply defined shape adroitly and compactly filled with motives.

124. Coil basket, Pima attribution, Arizona. The patterning and the basket shape are severe and controlled, the diagonals moving with authority and precision.

125. Coil basket, Pima attribution, Arizona. The diagonals bulge and waver, and the basket's shape lacks tension.

Anyone acquainted with the other textile arts who attempts to study basketry is immediately aware of the absence of systems of notation for designing. The only notations in basketry are for the analysis of existing baskets—for identification, classification, and understanding—and for help in learning to perform the different stitches. While comparable diagrams and analyses are common in weaving (in both basketry and weaving the constructions were originally developed through actual manipulations of the materials, while the drawings came *after)*, yet in weaving there are also systems of notation which made it possible to design textiles on paper. The designing, the precise devising of structural organizations, can be done away from the materials and mechanisms.

In weaving, the number of warp threads—or modular units—from selvage to selvage remains constant throughout the length of the piece, so that the total design can reasonably be figured out on graph paper. But in basketry the number of stakes—or modular units—constantly changes as the shape of the basket changes. A flared basket has many more modular units at its rim than at its base. It is very difficult to transcribe basketry patterns onto graph paper, or to work out on graph paper patterns to be transcribed in basketry. The problem is similar to that of expressing the relationships of the continents on a flat sheet of paper: a system that is successful at the equator is a disaster at the poles. Basketmaking has continued without methods of "designing" with sketches and diagrams and notations; it has continued without the need of making decisions in advance and recording them and then rendering the design. It has become most unusual in our society for any object to develop without sketches, even when the same person makes both the sketch and the object. Such plans vary from the rough sketch a painter makes on his canvas, laying out basic divisions and shapes, to the detailed cartoon of the tapestry weaver. When such sketches do not exist, there is a very strong tendency, as in basketry, to allow previous work to act as sketches. Not that baskets are always consciously copies, but something is made like something else, with only slight modifications or variations. This has been true of most basketry, so that baskets relate closely to those done before, and to those which will be done in the future.

Nowadays woven textiles can be designed away from the loom so precisely that the results are assured regardless of who sets up the loom. The resulting textiles show the influence of the new designing methods. The look of "drawing board design" is difficult to describe but it pervades all objects of our society. The shapes tend to show the mark of the instruments with which they were drawn on paper. They look as though they had been figured out on paper. They are without the spontaneous adjustments which a craftsman makes in developing a pattern through manipulating, watching, and modifying the materials. The results often seem dry and intellectual rather than visual or sensuous. This, of course, is an oversimplification; the distinctions are often extremely subtle.

Possibly basketry has never been subjected to design through notations on paper because it has always remained a hand process. The nearest approach to an engineering type of design in basketry is the melon-shaped basket which appeared in a how-to-do-it book for educators. The plan became an exercise in mechanical drawing. Even the words used to explain the drawing seem utterly foreign to basketry.

While the remnants of basket production which have persisted into the twentieth century seem anomalous and anachronistic, yet basketry has avoided the separation of the designer from his materials. Someone other than the basketmaker might sketch the silhouette of the proposed basket or specify a size and material or technique. Or a basketmaker might make a basket after a model. But the design itself always derives from the manipulation of the materials. When baskets seem at odds with the other things in our contemporary environment, we may attribute it to their being hand-made utilitarian objects in the midst of machine-made utilitarian objects. Their quality of differentness may derive also, and to a great measure, from their being the results of the ancient design methods of working directly with the materials, as opposed to modern approaches of working with ruler and pens on graph paper, or with symbols on a computer.

126. Diagram for constructing a melon-shaped basket. This approach is antithetical to the basketmaking procedures throughout history. (From The Basket Maker *by Luther Weston Turner)*

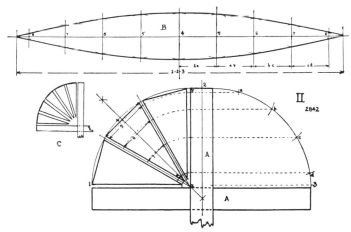

6 COILING

The Pima baskets on page 103 are coil baskets. Coiling, unlike other basketry techniques, is a process of sewing or stitching. Materials called the *foundation* are sewed together by a stitching element called the *binder*.

The foundation may be a single heavy reed or a group of such reeds, or a bundle of straw, or whatever is available. It is usually not like a length of yarn or cord made in advance, but is constituted all during the basketmaking, with new materials constantly added as the work progresses to maintain a foundation of the desired thickness. The foundation largely determines the thickness of the basket's walls. The finer the foundation, the thinner the walls, but also the slower the process. And the process is slow at best.

127. Coil basket for birdnest, Japan. Such baskets are quickly made with string as binder, with only enough stitches to hold the structure together.

128. Another view of Eskimo basket of plaited strips of kelp, Pt. Barrow (see Fig. 79). The plaited strips are prepared in advance and then sewn together into a basket.

129. Basket of plaited strips, Italy. After the strips are machine-sewn together, the basket is pressed into a mold to accomplish the scallops.

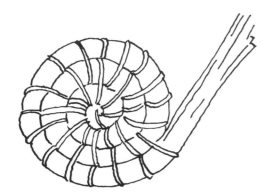

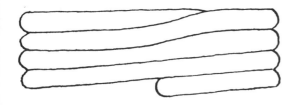

The spiral of the coil becomes a helix, with the foundation element always slightly tipped.

The foundation is continuous, spiraling from a center and continuing to the rim. Frequently the ending looks cut off somewhat arbitrarily, as though the foundation could just as well have continued endlessly. The spiral, or helix (when the coil moves upward to form a cylinder), has vigorous linear movement, with a beginning and an ending. It is not, as it may superficially appear, a series of concentric circles, or of stacked hoops. In moving from its beginning to its end, the single foundation element encompasses the entire basket.

A coil basket cannot be exactly symmetrical. Where the foundation moves from the base to begin the side walls it can be seen lifting off the horizontal base, upon itself, to move upward as a helix. At only one point on the circumference does the foundation lift from the base. From this point it rises in a continuous dynamic diagonal, never exactly parallel to the base, but always tipped at a slight angle, moving onward and upward. In a coil basket patterned with bands, the bands cannot encircle the basket and return where they started: each band must start lower than it ends. The heavier the foundation element and the smaller the circumference of the basket, the more pronounced the incline and the sense of departure from the symmetrical.

A coiled disc or mat seems to be a circle but it is not, even though the patterning implies a circle or symmetry. The disparity between the fact and what is implied creates its own tension. In ceramics, if a plate or bowl is decorated on a potter's wheel the banding can start and stop at the same point without a jog, just as the rim can be parallel to the base without a jog. But with coil basketry, the incline and the jog are facts which the pattern must in some way accommodate. And accommodations in pattern, as in structure, add visual interest and enrichment. An illustrator making a sketch of patterns on coil baskets would probably show them as circular or symmetrical, so slight is the departure from the circular or symmetrical. Yet the fact that patterns which in their essence are symmetrical appear on structures which in their essence are not symmetrical accounts for much of the visual quality of coil patterning.

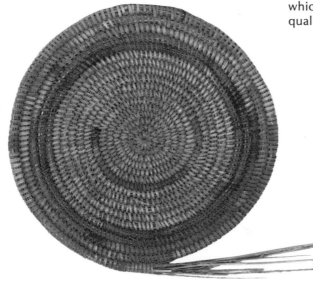

130. Unfinished coil basket, San Felipe Die-guenos, southern California. The foundation is not made in advance, but is added to as the basketry progresses. To maintain a foundation of uniform dimension, additions are made constantly.

131. Thick coil tray, Hopi, Arizona. The foundation is very small at the center, and increases
in dimension as the circumference increases.
The end is tapered to avoid a jog and to preserve the circular effect.

The stitching, or binding, material in coil baskets is a length of flexible grass or a narrow strip of palmetto or cord or similar material. Sometimes the stitching is done with a needle, but often the end of the "thread" is merely poked through holes which have been opened up with an instrument such as a sharpened bone. The stitching is pulled tight to hold the foundation rows close together. When the foundations are stitched tightly, the compression of the elements can make the baskets dense enough to hold liquids. Usually a coiled basket is very rigid. If instead it is allowed to be saggy or flexible, friction quickly wears out the binder, which, of course, is relatively slim and delicate.

The foundation can be laid down in any configuration and sewn together. The shape of the developing basket can be controlled by drawing in, or letting out, the foundation. The sides of the basket can rise vertically, or move out at angles or in curves. (The process and the shapes possible are noticeably like coil pottery. The coils of clay, of course, are held together with slip. The clay pot created from coils can be later modified and smoothed since the clay retains its plasticity until it dries, whereas in basketry no adjustment is possible after the coil is sewed.)

132. Coil basket, East Africa. The tipping of the coils is evident, as is the tapering of the foundation to avoid an abrupt ending.

The stitches must be close enough together not only to hold the foundation firmly in place, but also to keep the various bits of grasses or other short fibers which compose the foundation from falling out. If the materials composing the foundation are long, the stitching can be widely spaced, just close enough to hold the coils firmly in position. When the bundle is made up of short or delicate bits which, if exposed, would fall out or shatter and disintegrate, denser stitching is required. The foundation materials are not cohesive, and they are not spun or braided or knotted or in any way held together except by the stitching. Sometimes the binder is used for wrapping as well as stitching; it wraps around the foundation a number of times before it performs the conventional stitching together of adjoining coils. By such a combination of wrapping and stitching the binder can completely cover the foundation. Similarly, when the stitches are very close together the foundation can be seen only by forcing the stitches apart and looking between.

134. Coil basket of palm leaves, Korea. The binder is such a broad ribbon-like element that it completely covers the foundation.

135. Coil basket, Bamperde, Kasai District, Congo, Africa. The binder is unusually sparse, exposing the foundation throughout the basket. (Courtesy of the American Museum of Natural History)

When the surface of a coil basket is composed exclusively of the stitching element, the foundation acts like the warp in tapestry weaving, in which wefts completely cover warp, and the warp shows only as ridges creating highlights and shadows and generally activating the tapestry surface although the warp element itself is not seen. The appearance of patterning of coil baskets with their foundations completely covered is akin to the appearance of tapestry—the way the color changes are achieved, the way the surface elements lie parallel, and the way pure, unmodified colors are created.

136. Coil basket, Nubia. For short distances the binder wraps around the foundation without attaching to the adjoining foundation row. Stripes up the sides of the basket are created by these wrapped areas.

When the stitching is more widely spaced, the visual surface is created by the stitching elements in conjunction with the foundation, and any color of the stitching element is modified by the color of the foundation.

In all coil basketry the binder is on the exterior and interior surface of the basket, subject to all the wear. The sturdy bundle of the foundation is protected by the relatively delicate, flexible binder. Many old coil baskets show patches of stitching completely worn away, with the coarse foundation exposed.

Often the configuration of the stitching provides the basket's pattern. Sometimes stitches are split or spaced or varied in other ways. Sometimes the stitches are made to reach over three or four foundation rows to become long, fragile floats on the surface.

Suface decorations are applied over the coils during the stitching process. Strips of leather or rags or fragile colored glasses are laid along the outer surface of the foundation and held in place by the stitching. Sometimes shells, buttons, feathers, beads, etc. are affixed to the surface by the stitching. Such superstructural elements tend to conceal the foundation and provide the basket's color and texture. Of course, the pattern does not show on both the inside and outside. The baskets of the Northwest Coast are famous for imbricated surfaces in which superstructural elements are manipulated during the stitching process so that the stitching as well as the foundation is completely covered.

138. Coil basket, Nubia. The binder and the strips of leather which float on the surface create a checkerboard pattern.

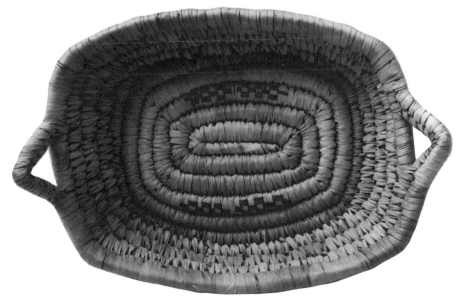

139. Coil basket, Tunisia. As a simple decoration in the bottom of the basket, colored strips of palm are laid on the surface of the foundation, and worked so that sometimes they lie over the binder. Similar patterning frequently appears on the rims of baskets.

140. Coil basket, Tunisia. Short strips of rag are laid on the surface of the foundation and held down by the binder. The strips are arranged in rough geometric patterns.

The coil technique has encouraged the kind of embellishment associated with embroidery. Since the sewing elements are short, usually the natural length of grasses and reed, they are constantly running out and new ones are started. If the materials happen to vary in color, they impart random color to the surface. Naturally, such variations have been accentuated and arranged in patterns. These patterns show on the inside of the basket as well as the outside, so that the basket seems patterned rather than covered with surface decoration.

141. Coil basket, India. The binder, which completely covers the coils, floats long distances on the surface, crossing over several foundation rows, to make colorful patterns.

The stitching can hold the foundation rows together very tightly, or it can space them so that openings exist between the rows as perforations. Such openings often serve utilitarian purposes, to allow water to drip out, or to lighten the weight of the basket. But sometimes the purpose is purely decorative. The appearance is lacelike, giving a sense of lightness, with intervals of open and closed, a sense of penetration of the basket walls; providing a simultaneous awareness of interior and exterior volume. The spacing of the foundation creates deeper shadows and stronger highlights. The surface becomes more active in its light reflectivity. Also, the foundation acquires a different identity—or it asserts its identity—as a spiral or helix. Elements become more individual, and the nature of the structure seems emphasized.

A marked feature of many coil baskets is the incredible regularity of the stitching—the spacing between stitches, the relationship of one row of stitches to the succeeding rows, especially the precise accommodations when the circumference changes from row to row, affecting the number of stitches and the relationships of the stitches to those on the preceding rows.

The regularity of stitches, although so often admired and commented upon, is less of a technical feat than is a smooth-flowing, energetic contour. The shapes of coil baskets are often their least interesting aspect. They frequently seem clumsy and uncertain. For the contour is created by the building of foundation row upon foundation row. In other basketry the contours may derive largely from elements bent and held in tension. In coil basketry, the contour derives from the precise placement of the foundation, which is then held with stitching. The slightest excess of coil makes a wavering or bulge in the contour. The basketmaker feels the curve in his fingertips and sensitively performs the most delicate adjustments of placing and holding the coil. Building the contour, like building the pattern, continues throughout the long basketmaking process and requires a remarkable continuity of precision.

Coil baskets have a special feel—of firmness, rigidity, solidity. They tend to settle down and almost become attached to the table or floor. When the foundation is very thick, the thickness of the basket's walls seems relatively clumsy in relation to the size of the basket, which has a chunkiness and solidity that can be very appealing. Of course, when the foundation is very thin, the walls are thin, with a special delicacy.

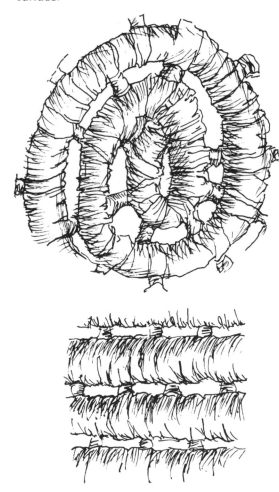

The coil technique in which the binder holds the foundation rows apart to create a perforated surface.

Several problems are peculiar to coil baskets. The point where the foundation commences, usually at the center of the base, is extremely difficult for the basketmaker. Often the center appears awkward or inappropriate. For if the foundation is at all thick or stiff, it resists being formed into a tight spiral, and a small hole is left at the center. Sometimes the beginning of the foundation is tapered to make possible a tighter center start. Sometimes the foundation is stitched at the center with so many stitches that the center becomes a different color from the overall color of the rest of the basket, and the center looks darned and overworked. Sometimes a small square of plaiting is used as a center, with the foundation sewn to the outer edge of the plaiting. A hole occurring at the center is sometimes covered with a piece of leather sewn in place by the same stitches that hold the foundation.

Certainly coil baskets are without the textile delight of elements supporting each other to create a textile membrane. Since the process is one of sewing elements together, a disparity usually exists between the relatively heavy foundation and the thin, flexible binder. The foundation element seems to *be* the basket, while the binder seems something holding the basket together, as slip holds the coil in coil pottery or as glue holds together the thin sheets of laminates. Even when the binding stitches are dense they seem to be mere decoration, covering the real structure.

143. Coil basket, Ovamboland, Africa. The basket starts with a rectangle of plaiting. The foundation increases in dimension as the work progresses.

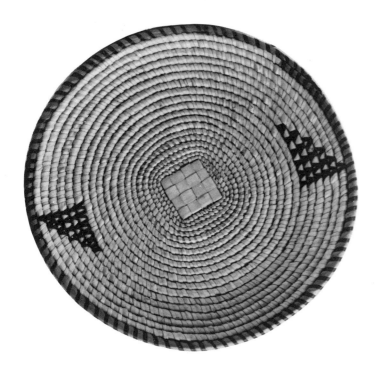

Coiling seems a simple form of basketry, easily comprehended and performed, especially insofar as small round mats are concerned. The process is slow, proceeding with great deliberation. It is especially conducive to superstructural decorative effects, which are often considered as less than pure expressions of the art of basketmaking.

Very occasionally a coiled basket shows a tenseness of shape, spontaneity, and directness which surmount the difficulties inherent in the process. Such a basket results from the most perfect control of the medium, from the greatest sensitivity in the laying down of the foundation. This control is maintained over days and weeks—or longer. Finally the basket emerges, and it appears so simple, so direct, so right, so inevitable.

The Paiute coil basket would generally be described as having black figures on a tan ground. Actually, both colors are mixtures showing the natural variations in the vegetal materials used for stitching and in the rods forming the foundation, which is barely visible between the stitches. The basket's bowl shape exposes the interior and exterior in such a way that both surfaces are seen simultaneously. Both show the pattern; the motifs seem not applied, but actually to be penetrating the thin, rigid walls. The hardness of the foundation creates such ridges, such highlights and shadows over the entire basket, that the pattern appears less well-defined than the black and tan description would suggest.

The patterning of American Indian baskets is seldom as sharply contrasting as we may have come to believe. The familiar, but unfortunate, renderings in flat colors which are so often used to show Indian motifs distort them by eliminating all the complex modulations and subtleties of color and texture (as well as the refinements of the silhouettes) which make the patterns work. These art renderings seem as remote from the visual facts as do the early English and French drawings, which we find so quaint today, that show the savages of the New World as naked Renaissance Europeans. Illustrators see the Indian motifs only in terms of our twentieth-century machine products. Our contemporary ideal of uniform, standardized color which can be repeated precisely for mass production is imposed even on what we see from the past. In our own products, color variations have come to be regarded as defects; consequently, irregularities in dye even in hand products can disturb us. At the same time, unexpected or illogical-seeming organizations of motifs are comprehensible only as mistakes. We sometimes patronizingly refer to them as errors, explaining that certain motifs "should have been" such and such. Similarly, our illustrations show the shapes as clean and streamlined. Thus, in describing, and even in seeing and thinking about such hand products, we modify them to make them conform to our own standards of machine uniformity and order.

Where the pattern commences toward the bottom of the basket, the coil row has 300 stitches. Where the pattern ends, toward the top, the coil row has 475 stitches. This increase in the number of stitches occurs gradually from row to row. The number of stitches per inch also varies slightly as the basketry progresses, so that at the top edge 104 stitches fill as much space as 100 stitches fill at the bottom. This means that the stitches are slightly closer together toward the top (like the *or nué*—shaded gold—technique in embroidery), making a most subtle variation from top to bottom. This almost imperceptible shading of a volume by gradations of color or texture is frequently practiced in ceramic glazing to define or accentuate shapes, providing implied shadows or highlights.

144. Coil basket, Paiute attribution, Nevada. The pattern appears on both inside and outside, and seems to penetrate the basket rather than to be a surface decoration.

The number of stitches changes from one row to the next not only because of the increasing circumference but because the basketmaker, consciously or unconsciously, spaced them closer together as the work progressed.

Within this changing number of stitches, the geometric pattern is constructed, constantly accommodating to the changing number of modular units available for creating the figure and ground. The problem is quite different from that of constructing geometric patterns with consistent numbers of units throughout the rows.

On close examination, the silhouette of this Paiute basket appears slightly bulgy and undulating rather than smooth. The bulges relate to the distribution of the pattern bands: the basket seems drawn in slightly at the top of each band. The basketmaker was obviously caught between increasing the stitches at a rate which would create a smooth silhouette, and increasing at a lesser rate consistent with the development of the motifs. The diamonds require a mirror or bilateral symmetry along both the vertical and horizontal axes. This is not possible when the number of modular units or stitches is constantly increasing as the basket enlarges. The basketmaker attempts to make the impossible seem not only possible but unexceptional. A basket showing both a regular geometric pattern precisely related to the changing number of stitches and a smooth vigorous silhouette in the basket shape is a remarkable achievement.

PLAITING

The Sarawak baskets are diagonal plaiting. They consist entirely of diagonal elements intersecting at right angles. There is no distinction between the elements, as warp and weft, or as foundation and binder. All elements perform the same function; all are equally active.

The elements for plaiting tend to be flat, ribbon-like, flexible, and cohesive. All must interact in the structure; none can remain static and inflexible while others move around it.

The ribbon-like flatness and flexibility are essential to a tight interweaving. Unless they are flat and flexible they will not fit together but will hold themselves apart, with openings left between. The thinness and the flexibility which are essential to tight interweaving impart a sense of fragility to the basket, and a sense of its being clothlike. Plaited baskets conform more than other baskets to general ideas of "textiles." The construction seems like the thinnest membrane, a sort of interface between interior and exterior volumes. The baskets seem to be delicate, to require special holding and handling, as though they would be deformed by the slightest pressure, or torn by the slightest mishandling. They often seem at odds with the definition of baskets as "hard" textiles. They feel delicate and malleable in contrast to the solidity and rigidity of tight coiling in coil baskets, or the firmness of willow or reed in wickerwork baskets.

145. Plaited baskets, Sarawak, Borneo. The basket at the top shows the use of supports at the base and rim, and up the sides. The other basket has the side supports extended as legs lifting the contents off the ground. (Courtesy of the American Museum of Natural History)

146. Plaited baskets, Sarawak, Borneo. The basket at the left is of fairly rigid, less ribbon-like elements which do not fit tightly together but make a perforated surface. The other basket is soft and flexible, with no rigid supports. The dark elements can be seen spiraling up the sides. (Courtesy of the American Museum of Natural History)

147. Plaited baskets, Madagascar and India. The basket in the foreground, from Madagascar, shows how the elements can be pulled in plaiting to force the corners into points. The basket from India is plaited into an extravagant shape. (See also Figs. 159 and 160.)

Plaited baskets tend to be square at the base, with rather pronounced corners. The base is often saucer-like; the corners seem to want to lift off the ground—so different from the coil baskets, which seem to settle down flat. Even in the way plaited baskets rest on the surface they express their lift, their buoyancy, their lightness.

As the plaited basket continues upward from the base, the shape quickly turns cylindrical, so that the top rim is a circle. Frequently the sides indent slightly, or bulge out. The transition from square to round occurs gradually, creating a volume of exceeding beauty, aglow with subtle shadows and highlights.

A tall plaited cylinder can become like a soft tube of cloth, unable to support itself. Consequently, such baskets are frequently reinforced with stiff vertical rods lashed to the sides. Often, too, the rim and base are reinforced with hoops or other supporting and strengthening devices. The reinforcement at the base counteracts the basket's tendency to become saucer-like, and ensures that the basket will sit securely. The supports attached to the sides are often allowed to extend beyond the base to create legs so that the basket is lifted from the surface on which it is placed. The contents are thus kept off the damp ground.

In all basketry the accommodations are fascinating features—whether the accommodation is to force a motif into the shape as it develops, or to make a symmetrical pattern appear on a non-symmetrical structure, or to strengthen a weak basket, or to allow it to sit securely.

Plaited baskets, even when very lightweight, can define a large interior volume. A large plaited basket is light to carry; it adds almost nothing to the weight of the load. It is so flexible it can often be folded compactly until needed. And even when it is extremely light, the structure can be dense enough to hold fine particles; sometimes the structure is dense enough to hold water. The actual basketmaking is fast. Even a large basket can be quickly fabricated. Of course, the wider the ribbon-like elements, the faster the basketmaking.

148. Plaited basket, Philippine Islands. The rim is reinforced with a wide strip of bamboo. The basket seems inflated. The saucer-like base forces the corners to lift from the table surface. See also Fig. 219.

149. Plaited baskets, Sarawak, Borneo. The first basket is a long, flexible sleeve in simple over-one, under-one plaiting. The two others are twill plaiting, with variations at the bases and rims. (Courtesy of the American Museum of Natural History)

150. Plaited lid of a large bamboo storage basket, Philippine Islands. The luster of the bamboo emphasizes the twill pattern and the subtle curving of the plaited surface.

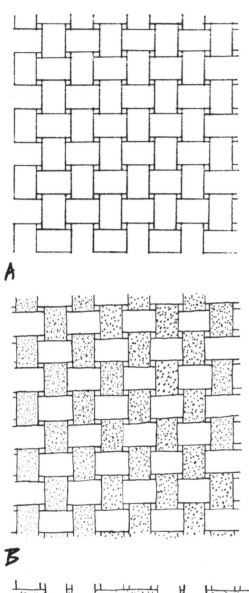

A

B

C

(A) Over-one, under-one plaiting with identical materials, (B) Over-one, under-one plaiting with the two systems in different colors, (C) Twill plaiting, over-two, under-two, with the two systems in different colors.

The basic structure of plaiting is over-one, under-one. This limits the patterning possibilities to those of plain weave in weaving. Colors can appear in bands and stripes, or in checkerboards when a system of light elements intersects a system of dark elements. When the plaited structure departs from the over-one, under-one system, the potential for patterning is greatly increased. When the structural elements are floated over two, or over three, many patterns are created. Unfortunately, as the float increases in length, the number of intersections (where an element of one system moves through the other system) is reduced—and it is the number of intersections which holds the two systems tightly together. The floating elements tend to lift off the textile surface slightly; they thus regain their vulnerability as unsupported single thicknesses, and they become susceptible to catching and tearing. In order to increase the structural soundness of floating elements, the widths of the ribbon-like elements must be narrowed to reduce the length of the float.

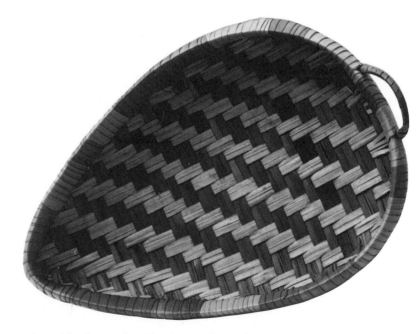

151. Plaited basket, India. The diagonals established by twill plaiting are emphasized by having a dark system cross a light system.

152. Plaited basket, Alaska. The plaited ribbons of bark are not on the diagonal but are weft elements moving through warps as in wickerwork. The pattern results not only from differences in color but also from occasional changes in the weaving.

153. Detail of plaited basket, Alaska. Sometimes the weft, instead of going over-one, under-one, floats over two warps, or three, or four. Yet the total effect is of a compact interlacing.

154. Detail of hexagonal plaiting, plaited hat, Malacca, Malaysia. In this type of plaiting, three systems of elements, rather than the usual two, intersect to form a surface which seems constructed of tiny cubes.

155. Plaited basket, Luzon, Philippine Islands. The relatively rigid elements float long distances to create a damask pattern. The surface is protected by a number of exterior supports which seem to frame the more fragile plaiting.

156. Plaited basket, Hopi, Arizona. The plaiting of this yucca basket is over-three, under-three. In order to make a pattern with mirror symmetry, the floats are sometimes lengthened still further. See also Fig. 223.

157. Detail of plaited basket, India. The hexagonal plaiting is elaborated by twisting the elements into rolls on the surface.

In plaited basketry as in weaving, the number of patterns possible within a sound structure is increased when the elements are fine. And fine elements take more time in the preparation and in the construction. The results tend toward greater refinement in appearance, perhaps less vigor and spontaneity. As baskets become less utilitarian and more ceremonial-decorative, the complex patternings in plaiting become feasible. But for the work baskets with rather wide elements, the patterning is restricted to plain-weave effects, or to patterns created out of short floats.

There is wonder in taking paper-thin strips, and manipulating them into a continuous membrane, never thicker than the thickness of two strips—without gaps or holes or seams—just a continuous membrane, formed into the basket shape. And sometimes that membrane is patterned. No gaps, no holes, and no seams.

158. Plaited basket, India. The total basket seems an elaboration of the hexagonal shapes created by the hexagonal plaiting.

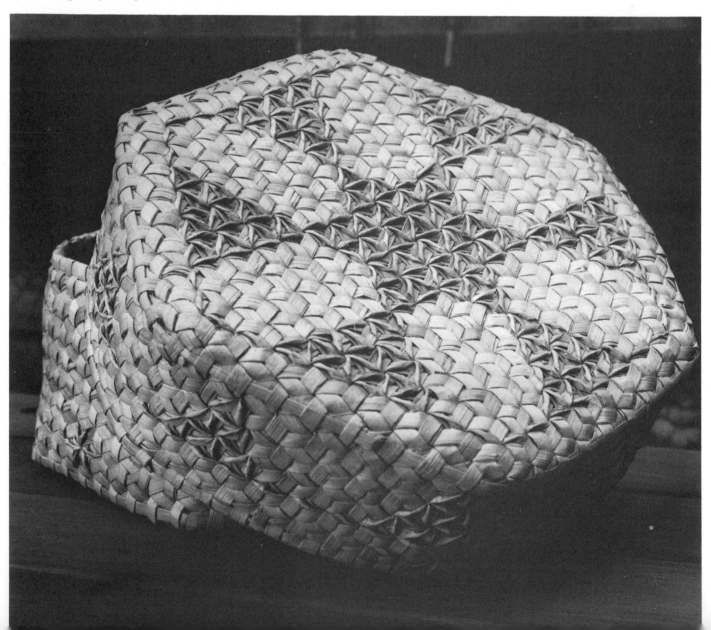

159. Plaited basket, India. The outer layer of plaited elements is perforated with round holes under which metal foil is inserted to glitter over the intricate surface.

160. Another view of plaited basket, India. The base of this so-called Taj Mahal basket starts with six elements which form a sort of warp, with others added as the work progresses.

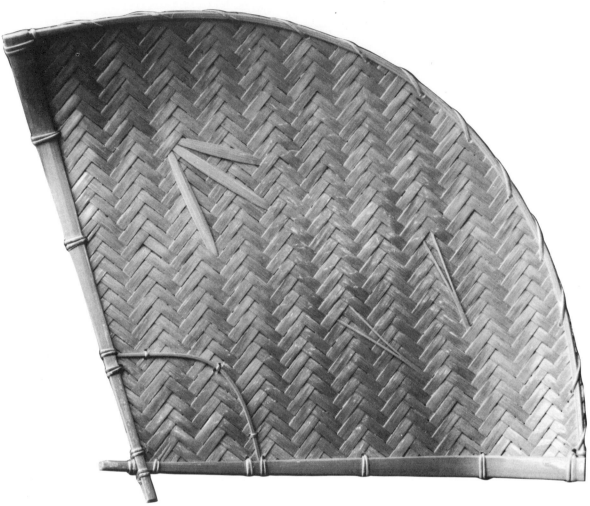

161. Bamboo tray, Japan. A sheet of plaiting is cut into a fan shape and the edges protected with shaped strips which accentuate the fan. Bamboo strips, like embroidery, are laid on the surface with their ends inserted into the plaiting.

162. Plaited bamboo basket covered with gold paper, Japan. The large openings are filled in by the paper. The sheen of the paper emphasizes the plaited structure and even the nodes of the bamboo.

164. Plaited bamboo basket, Japan. The nodes of the bamboo are carefully arranged to create a decorative band at the center of the cylinder.

163. Basket of plaiting and wickerwork, Luzon, Philippine Islands. This elegant fish basket takes the shape of a wickerwork and twined basket except in the upper section, where the ribbon-like elements are twill-plaited and cut into an irregular opening.

165. Plaited palm basket, Tunisia. The basket appears to be wide plaited strips sewn together. Actually, the plaiting is performed during the basketmaking, and the strips are joined together through the plaiting itself.

The basket from Colombia is plaited from narrow split strips of reed- or canelike elements with their glossy exterior kept on the basket's outer surface. Because of the hardness and relative inflexibility of the material—in contrast to palm and flax which are also often plaited—the elements are held slightly apart at each intersection. They refuse to fit tightly together. Had they been plaited in an over-one, under-one order, the openings would have been more frequent and more pronounced. But the basket is plaited over-three, under-three, which reduces the number of intersections and allows the individual elements to fit together more tightly. Because the plaiting is on the diagonal, all the checkerboard squares are tipped, while the twill (which in weaving runs diagonally across a piece of cloth) runs horizontally.

166. Plaited basket, Amazon region, Colombia. The dark and light elements are grouped to create a bold checkerboard. At the base a tighter structure is achieved through twill plaiting.

167. Another view of plaited basket, Amazon region, Colombia. The concentric rectangles at the base are achieved by staining each element dark halfway down its length.

136

A casual examination of the basket suggests that certain elements are colored brown, while others are left their natural tan, and that a system of brown elements intersects a system of tan elements. If this were true, the pattern created would not be the concentric squares which show on the base of the basket. The distribution of brown and tan would have to appear as in the accompanying sketch, with a sort of fracturing of the squares. Such fractured patterns are common in plaited basketry showing two colors. To produce the concentric squares in the Colombian basket, the basketmaker resorted to a subtle device. He colored the outer side of each element brown for only half its length, and left the remainder tan. This refinement is imperceptible unless an element is traced through the basket or unless the observer is familiar with the patterns possible in plaiting dark and light elements.

The twill plaiting of the base is over-three, under-three. When the twill moves up the sides, the dark and light show as bands encircling the basket. Then the woven pattern is changed to basket weave, with four elements moving together to cross four elements, to create the bold checkerboard set on the diagonal. At the rim the 3-3 twill returns. The elements are folded over at the top, keeping the cut edges inside the basket. The rough edges are held down with a heavier strip, while another strip encircles the outside of the rim. These reinforcing hoops, inside and outside the basket, are lashed together.

The basket is round at the rim and square at the base; the shape between, as it moves from the square to the circle, appears inflated. Because of the stiffness of the elements, the basket has a certain rigidity. With its reinforcing hoops at the rim, it is sturdy and easy to handle. It is light and springy. It seems bold and straightforward—deceptively straightforward, for the direct-appearing pattern could not have been achieved without the refined device of elements of discontinuous color.

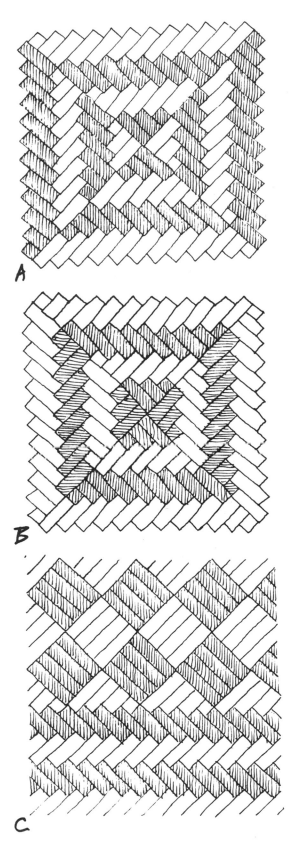

(A) Plaited base as it would appear if the two systems were of different colors, (B) Plaited base as it appears because all the elements change color halfway down their length, (C) The twill plaiting changes to basketweave to create a large checkerboard effect.

8

TWINING & WICKERWORK

The third basic structure of basketry is that in which a system of warps, or stakes, is held together by wefts. A single weft can move round and round through the stakes in an over, under pattern called *wickerwork*. Or two or more wefts can move together, twisting as they go and locking a stake in each twist, in what is called *twining*. All sorts of variations in wickerwork and twining are possible. Each produces a different visual and tactile surface. Patterns on baskets are often created not through changes in color or material but by the "weaves." Bands of wickerwork are set against bands of twining for subtle effects. Sometimes these changes are purely decorative, but often their purpose is structural. A row of twining, for instance, locks the warps tightly and holds them firm and in precise position, so that such a row often occurs at crucial points in the basketry—at extreme changes in direction; when the stakes are being forced into regular spacing at the base; at the rim; etc.

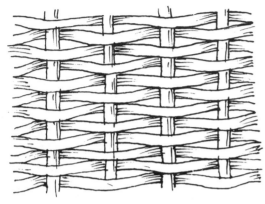

Wickerwork.

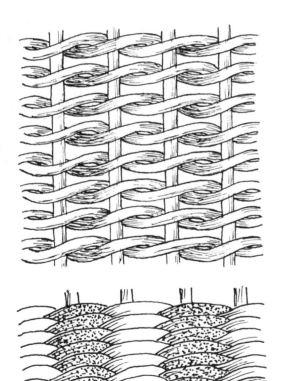

Twining.

168. Wickerwork basket, Iroquois. Such a basket of ribbon-like hickory splints as warp and weft seems to be plaiting as much as wickerwork. The basket is rectangular at the base, yet circular at the rim. The unusual shape at the neck is achieved by tapering the warp elements.

169. Unfinished wickerwork basket, Great Andaman, Andaman Islands. The base has already
been dented in so that the basket will sit on a
flat surface.

170. Wickerwork basket, Peru. The flexible warps intersect, two by two, which creates the basketweave base.

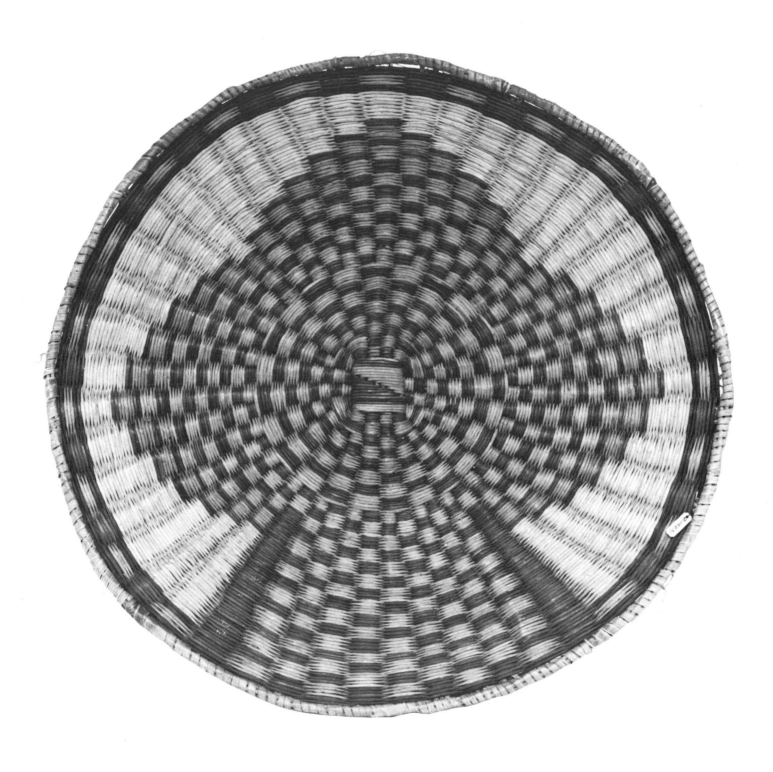

172. Wickerwork basket, Hopi, Arizona. This
deep basket is like a Hopi tray forced into a
basket shape. The start at the base (see Fig.
208) is similar to the overlapping at the center
of the Hopi trays. The disparity between the dimensions of warp and weft is minimized by
grouping the weft colors.

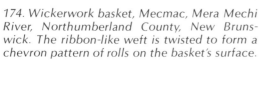

174. *Wickerwork basket, Mecmac, Mera Mechi River, Northumberland County, New Brunswick. The ribbon-like weft is twisted to form a chevron pattern of rolls on the basket's surface.*

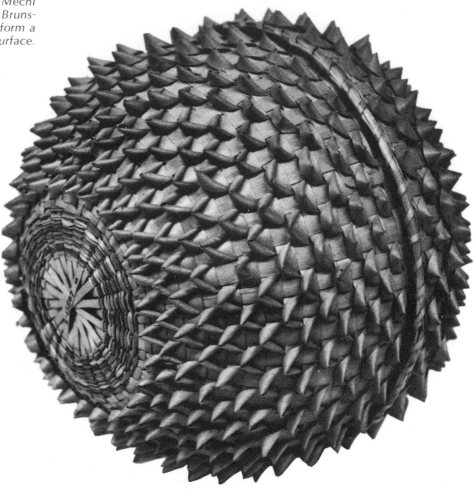

175. *Wickerwork basket, Mecmac, Mera Mechi River, Northumberland County, New Brunswick. Like the basket in Fig. 174, this one has its weft moving out of the structure in a loop. Here the surface decoration turns the basket into a sort of pinecone.*

176. Bamboo wickerwork basket, China. The weft moves over wide slat-like warps to create a very smooth surface.

177. Twined storage basket, Suku, Congo, Africa. The wide warps are held together by widely spaced twining.

178. Twined basket, Attu, Aleutian Islands. The twining, like that in the basket from Suku, Congo, is spaced and, in this instance, forms perforations in the flexible basket. The pattern is worsted yarn in many colors.

179. Twined basket, Peru. The banding is achieved by a change in the twining, which occurs also at the base and at the top of the cover to define the change in direction.

180. Twined Tlingit basket, Juneau, Alaska.
The colorful bands of patterning on the brown
basket are called "false embroidery."

181. Twined basket, Yurok, northern California. This openwork basket for storing mush spoons has a pattern of crossed warps moving up the sides and around the top.

182. Twined basket, Ghana. This flexible basket
is twined with cord, which is also used as a
binding element at the handle and rim.

183. Twined seed-fan, Pah-tin, Colusa, California. The twining acts to separate the warps and hold them securely in a sturdy, rigid construction.

184. Wickerwork and twined baskets from the Philippine Islands and Japan. The uncompleted basket is an example by the author to show the tactile surfaces created by various twinings, and the sense of movement of warps through the construction as their numbers increase.

185. Bottom of wickerwork basket, Korea (see also Figs. 92 and 96). It is evident how the warps are arranged in flat, ribbon-like elements moving together, how they divide as the circumference increases, and how additions are made.

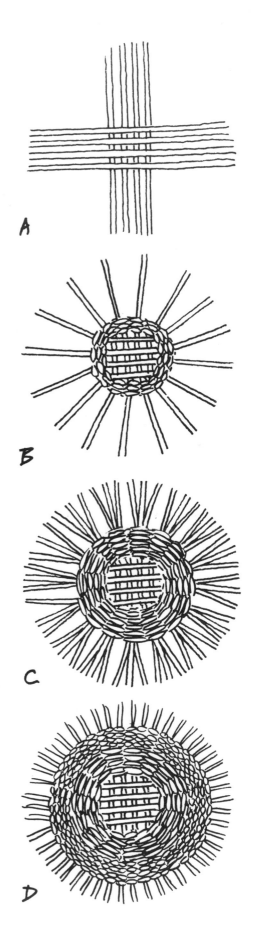

(A) Warp elements are intersected, four over four, (B) Warps are held in place and spread apart by twining, (C) Additional stakes are added, (D) The twining continues through the total number of stakes. The length of the twined stitch changes where the number of warps increases, and creates a slight tactile change in the twined surface.

In establishing a system of warps for this kind of basketry, a number of elements overlap or intersect at the point which will become the center of the base. Many ingenious methods have been devised to keep this center from becoming thick and clumsy and without awkward holes. The first rows of weft hold the stakes in place, in order, and force them to lie in a plane. As the circle of weaving grows larger, more stakes may be added to avoid having the stakes too widely separated as the circumference of the basket increases. An interaction usually occurs between the warp stakes and the wefts, as between the warps and wefts in the weaving of cloth. But sometimes the wefts do all the accommodating. Sometimes the warps are completely covered by the wefts. At other times, areas of warp are exposed for long distances.

186. Wickerwork basket, Mexico. Flat strips overlap at the center, with a heavy, tough weft forcing them into a flat plane.

Twined and wickerwork baskets can be as rigid as the familiar willow baskets, or as soft and flexible as some of the fine Aleutian Island baskets. The shapes of the baskets are frequently vigorous and direct, created by the bent elements which form the stakes, held in position by the wefts.

If four rods cross four rods at right angles to start a basket, the number of stakes—sixteen—is immediately established. From then on the work, including the finishing edge, is in relation to the sixteen. As the weft is inserted, these original stakes become evenly spaced. Then, as the circumference increases, the sixteen radiating spokes move farther and farther apart. Unless more are added, the basket becomes weak and flimsy, or the wefts pack more and more closely together. Stakes must then be added in relation to the original sixteen. For the very uniform baskets which we use in our everyday lives—the baskets made by craftsmen for export from Hong Kong, Taiwan, Yugoslavia, stakes are seldom added one here, one there, as needed. Usually sixteen additional stakes are added at once, with one inserted alongside each existing stake.

189. Twined basket, Yurok, northern California. This jumping-dance basket has twined sides like a sheet of matting folded and finished with leather ends and rim.

190. Basket of twining and wickerwork, probably Taiwan. Warps are crossed, and on the rim are plaited, to form an openwork pattern.

If new stakes were to be inserted at irregular intervals, as they are in many American Indian baskets of twigs, the shape of the work would tend to become irregular. The surface would buckle or ripple because the order would be disturbed. The already existing elements would react irregularly to compensate for the irregular additions. When uniform elements are manipulated uniformly, they tend to take a regular shape. The rippling effect can be seen in the Yurok-Karok tobacco basket in which stakes were added at irregular intervals to increase and decrease the circumference. In the areas where the number of stakes changes, the shape loses its tenseness; it looks somewhat puckered, gathered in. The shape implies a softness and flexibility greater than that actually possessed by the basket.

In the Karok basket of hazel twigs the additional stakes occur in no regular order. The result is an appearance of irregularity throughout the basket, rather consistent with the hazel, which is irregular and appears difficult to manipulate. The observer in looking at the basket is aware of the problems: the process did not seem to proceed easily and surely, but required constant decisions and adjustments.

The optimum distance between stakes is determined by the gauge of the elements, and the type and function of the construction. Increasing and decreasing the number of stakes to maintain this optimum spacing as the shape increases and decreases accounts for much of the surface beauty of basketry shapes. The warps move through the wefts like veins, separating and merging, with the wefts reacting as they must, the length of the stitches constantly changing from weft row to weft row.

191. Twined tobacco basket, Yurok-Karok, northern California. The twining with dark and light elements creates subtle bands of pattern.

192. *Twined openwork food tray of hazel, Karok, northern California. In such an openwork construction, the addition of elements as the circumference increases is most evident. The twining holds all these irregular hazel twigs firmly in place.*

The Yugoslavian basket is constructed of brown willow which is split, showing a brown shiny outside and a white dull inside. The brown appears on the outside of the basket and on the inside center, while the white shows in the reverse areas. The contrast of shiny and dull texture, and of brown and white color, is always apparent because of the basket's shape and open construction. The sense of contrast is carried still further by the marked difference between the open and closed areas formed by the various weaves.

The starting stakes or spokes are not split. Being cylindrical rods, they are stiff and form a sturdy, rigid base. They terminate just before the openwork commences in the upward curve. There the flatter and more flexible split willows are substituted for the original rods.

Four rods intersect four others at right angles, a most common way of starting a basket. The rods do not overlap, four upon four, as it may appear, but instead the second group of four moves through slits in the first four. Such an intersection holds the stakes firm until the wefts can keep them in position. Now sixteen stakes radiate from the center, and since an odd number is required for the weaving, a seventeenth stake is added. When enough weft is woven to form a flat disc of the desired size, the original stakes are cut off at the edge of the weaving. Two stakes of split willow are then inserted on each side of the original stakes and forced down well into the woven structure. A row of four-rod twining of relatively fine willow is put in at this point to hold the new stakes firm and to form a slight foot on

193. Wickerwork basket, Yugoslavia. The brown exterior of the split willow shows as a disc in the center of the basket's interior.

the bottom of the basket, like the foot on most dinner plates, so that it will sit well on a table.

There are now sixty-eight stakes as ribs for the sides of the basket. The even number is necessary for the crossed-warp technique. While seventeen and sixty-eight may seem capricious and random numbers, they evolved logically from the original four crossing four and the subsequent requirements of the weaves.

At the rim the ribs are held firmly in place, before they are cut off, by a row of twining which is not visible in the finished basket because a strip of split willow is added on both the inside and outside, encasing the twining. The clipped ends are cushioned by a braid of softer, grassy fiber lying along the top edge. All this bundle at the rim is bound together firmly with a split willow. The result is a rim big enough to be held comfortably in the fingers. There are no exposed ends; everything is secure, and the tactile sensation is pleasant. All the parts that the hands contact in using the basket are smooth, glossy surfaces.

Although the basket appears simple, yet it employs a succession of techniques. All elements are structural. The marked decorative sense arises from the material itself as it appears in structural techniques.

Numerous other ways have been devised to construct baskets. All are interrelated, intermixed. Each kind of construction flows imperceptibly into the next to create the large category of objects called baskets.

194. Another view of wickerwork basket, Yugoslavia.

195. Raffia basket, Ischia, Italy. The wire frame is heavily wrapped so that it seems padded.

A few of these other methods seem especially worthy of mention. The Ischia basket is built over a wire frame or armature. The frame by itself shows the shape of the basket. The raffia merely fills in the openings. The fillings are simple all-over patterns and individual motifs. Some are worked in red and green against the natural raffia color. The raffia serves to keep things from falling out of the basket and provides a pleasant tactile sensation, beyond its purely decorative quality. The patterns and motifs are repeated over and over in the thousands of such baskets—yet some of these Ischia baskets achieve a remarkable freshness and vigor, even a sense of individuality and spontaneity.

The baskets from Colombia and from Spain are similar in appearance to the Ischia baskets. They are formed from wire components which the basketmaker assembles in the basketry process. The diamond is only a bent wire: its ends are not even soldered together. This diamond is elaborated and held together with basketry; then it is affixed inside the oval, again held together with basketry and elaborated. The sides are a length of wire bent into scallops, with taller scallops for the handles of the basket. Such an assembling of components is quite unusual among basket techniques.

196. Basket built of wire components, Spain. A delicate lacelike pattern fills all the openings, while the wire foundation provides the rigidity and support.

The melon-shaped willow basket from Greece is so basic in design that the identical shape in identical materials appears in numerous parts of the world. The basket is distinguished by its round, compact, sturdy shape, with decorative motifs (similar to the currently popular God's eyes) at the joinings of the handle and rim. These diamond shapes, which might be mistaken for superstructural surface decorations, are in fact essential to the basket's structure.

The basket starts with a length of willow rod bent into a hoop to become the handle. In this particular example the ends of this sturdy rod are tapered where they overlap each other, and are held together with a wire. Because willow rods are amazingly strong and springy, holding such elements to the hoop shape is difficult. So wire is used, or a small tack is inserted through the overlapping ends. A second hoop is similarly formed to become the border of the basket. This is slipped over the first hoop and lashed in place with split willow, which forms the decorative diamonds.

Melon-shaped basket. (A) A hoop is formed and (B) crossed by another hoop. These two hoops are (C) held in position at their junctures. (D) Ribs are placed under tension between the diamonds. Weft is then interlaced, starting at both diamonds and meeting in the middle.

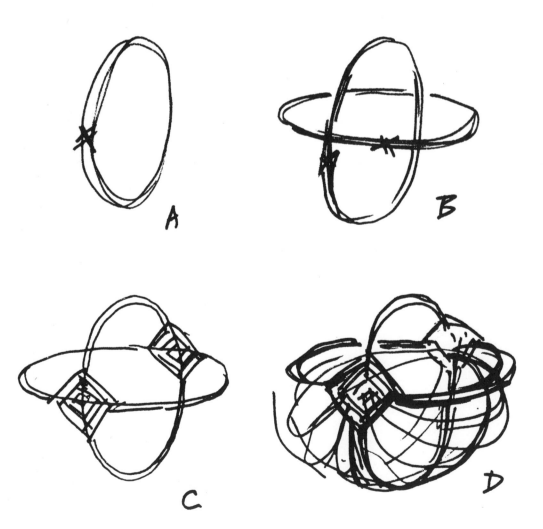

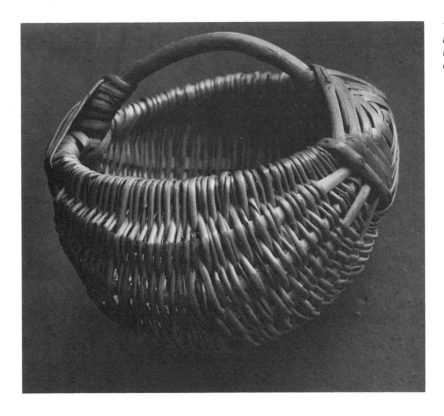

197. Melon-shaped willow basket, Greece. The heavy skeleton is filled in with thinner elements; the meeting of the weft filling is evident at the center.

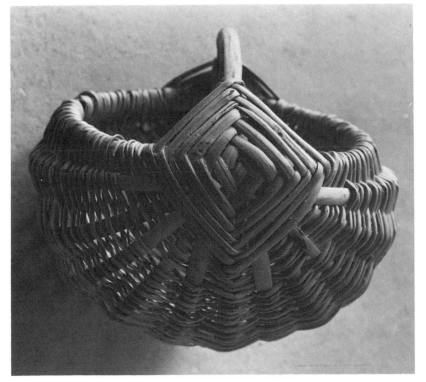

198. Another view of melon-shaped willow basket, Greece. The diamond-shaped patterns at the ends of the handle hold the rim and handle together to start the basketmaking.

199. Melon-shaped willow basket, Yugoslavia. The melon-shape has been modified to make a flatter, shallower basket able to sit upright on a flat surface.

Such sturdy willow as that of the hoops is often soaked for several days before it is used, to make it pliable. When soaked, willow is remarkably flexible, but then it rapidly dries out, even during the forming process, and becomes quite rigid. The split willow which forms the decorative diamonds is also flexible when added to the construction, but it quickly becomes dry and stiff and acts as diagonal bracing which holds the hoops in position at right angles to each other. Even at this early point in the process, without any weft, all the elements are rigid and securely held. A few lengths of split willow are then tapered at their ends, bent into a curve, and installed in position as ribs, where they stay because the springiness of the rods keeps their ends pushed against the insides of the diamond shapes. A few wefts are interwoven, and then the remaining ribs are added. The final wefts are interwoven from the two sides toward the middle. The meeting of the wefts in the center of the basket is apparent in the photograph.

200. Willow baskets, Spain. The heavy willow works as a sort of skeleton into which the flexible split strips are worked as weft to fill the openings.

This basketry process, then, starts with the handle and rim and ends with the middle wefts. The wefts function to fill in the openings between the ribs and to hold the ribs in place. They do little to determine the curve of the ribs. The skeleton of the basket—the handle, rim, and ribs—is a sort of rigid armature covered over, as though with a skin of flexible and delicate wefts. The method of construction exploits the properties of willow: its potential to become flexible and then rigid; its enormous resilience; its woodiness, which allows it to be whittled into shape and split into elements of various sizes. The satin glossiness of willow's outer surface is displayed especially in the half-rounds which lie parallel to each other for long unbroken distances. This length gives the maximum sensation of shine. Set at right angles to each other, the willow elements create a juxtaposition of shiny and dull according to the angle of the light, making the diamond motifs active in the reflection of light.

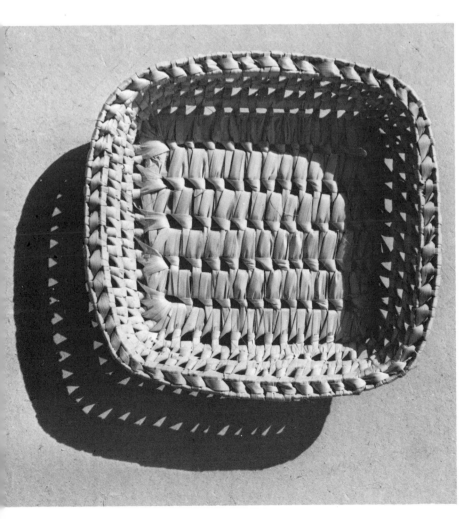

201. Palm fiber basket, Portugal. The basket shows foundation elements held together by a broad binder to form open spaces.

202. *Bamboo basket, Japan. The elements are in a complex organization which combines plaiting, twining, and wickerwork.*

203. *Detail of bamboo basket, Japan. The strips of bamboo float for long distances to create a lustrous surface.*

Like everything else in the textile arts, baskets defy satisfactory classification. Even the category "baskets" is not precise. These objects flow imperceptibly into boxes and bags and mats and weavings. Distinctions become arbitrary and unclear. Finally what prevails from a survey of baskets is not a sense of neat classes of products, but an awareness of man throughout the world and throughout the centuries creating with infinite skill and ingenuity and delight, with reverence and gentleness, manipulating many various materials in many various ways to make many varied objects to satisfy many varied needs.

205. Plaited basket, India. The ribbon-like elements in bright colors are worked into plaited modular units composed into an eccentric basket shape.

BASKETRY STRUCTURE

9

When the Andaman Islanders take a number of reeds and tie them into a star form, they are using a fast method of forcing stakes to radiate from a center. This method has distinct disadvantages: the clumsy overlapping of reed upon reed makes a thick, rounded center which keeps the egg-shaped basket from sitting upright on a flat surface. In a hunting shelter such a basket can hang from the roof, but in other situations the round bottom is inconvenient.

With this fast method of starting, only at some distance from the center can the stakes be forced into a position side by side, and a weft inserted to hold the stakes in place. Consequently, open spaces and gaps result at the bottom of the basket, exactly where they are most impractical. Also, with the clumsy tying, a smooth interior surface cannot be achieved.

Despite the disadvantages of this fast method of starting, there is an appealing directness in having all the stakes easily traceable from the center to their termination at the border—indeed, traceable from the border down to the center and back up to the border on the opposite side—as though each stake expresses the arching silhouette of the basket and as though, if a single arched element revolved, it would define the entire basket.

206. Basket from Little Andaman, similar to basket in Fig. 11. The round warps cannot form a flat center. Only at a considerable distance from the overlapping can weft be introduced; consequently, the bottom of the basket has large openings.

207. Wickerwork basket from North Andaman Island (see also Fig. 74). A bundle of warps is tied together to start the basket. Only gradually can they be separated and weft introduced. The first wefts must be widely separated.

208. Wickerwork basket, Hopi, Arizona (see also Fig. 172). The basket, like the Hopi trays, commences with a sort of strap of warps worked together to cross another strap of warps.

In many plaited baskets a similar continuation of each warp occurs from border to border. And when the plaiting is on the diagonal, every element used in the basket takes this border-to-border configuration. This feature is not especially obvious because the individual elements are not so easily traced through the structure as are the warps in the Andaman Island baskets. The surface appears as a mosaic of tipped squares with no clear continuity from one to the next, except when, as frequently occurs, a random element of another color appears in a basket which is otherwise monochrome. The configuration of the element is then apparent. It seems to spiral down the basket and back up again, sometimes crossing over itself in the process. It seems to define more than just the silhouette—in itself it defines the total three-dimensional volume, the total space being enveloped or enclosed by the basket.

An overlapping of stakes at the center similar to that of the temporary Andaman Island basket, although without the tying, frequently occurs in permanent baskets when the stakes are flat, thin elements such as split bamboo and cane. In such instances the individual stakes are carefully arranged for the maximum thinness and smoothness at the base. But when the stakes are more or less round in cross-section, other methods are used to achieve radiation of spokes from a center.

In some of the temporary baskets the makers used as "starts" the constructions which occur in nature. Palm leaves proved especially convenient, with their leaflets securely attached either to a center, as in a fan palm, or to a rib, as in a coconut palm. Nature seemed to dispose the leaves for interweaving. When the natural distribution of leaflets did not provide enough elements for the density of plaiting desired, sometimes several fronds were overlapped to double or triple the number of leaflets.

209. Twined basket, Mexico. Groups of three elements lie parallel to act as single warps. These intersect at the center, and only at some distance from this center can a twined weft hold them in order and in a plane.

171

210. *Plaited basket, Philippine Islands. The center is similar to that of the Mexican twined basket, yet here the ends of elements are all disposed to end halfway from the center to the rim.*

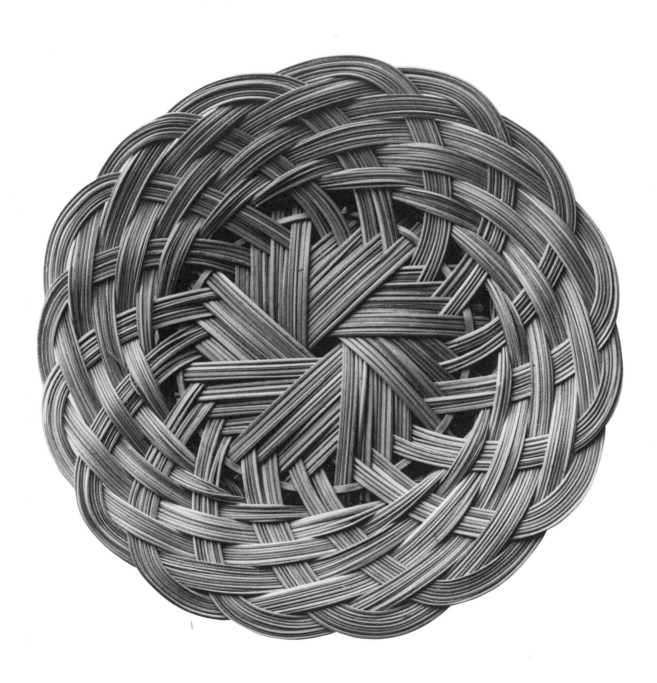

172

211. Cane basket, Mexico. This large basket uses flattened cane as very broad warp elements which overlap at the center in a thick mass of warp upon warp.

With elements that are unattached and separate, the start is more difficult than when they are tied together as in the Andaman Island basket, or when the natural growth pattern holds several linear elements together. To an unusual degree the basketmaker imposes his will upon the materials when he first holds them together with his hands, or with his heel, and forces them into a configuration of interrelationship. He establishes a precisely ordered organization from elements which seem willfully inclined to retain their own separate individuality. The basketmaker seems to need more hands to get the work started. Elsewhere in the basket, after some of the elements are firmly held together, they all seem more compliant.

212. Fishing basket, Sicily. Overlapping bundles of warps compose the center. The "weft" is a wire which spirals from the center and is lashed to the crossed warps.

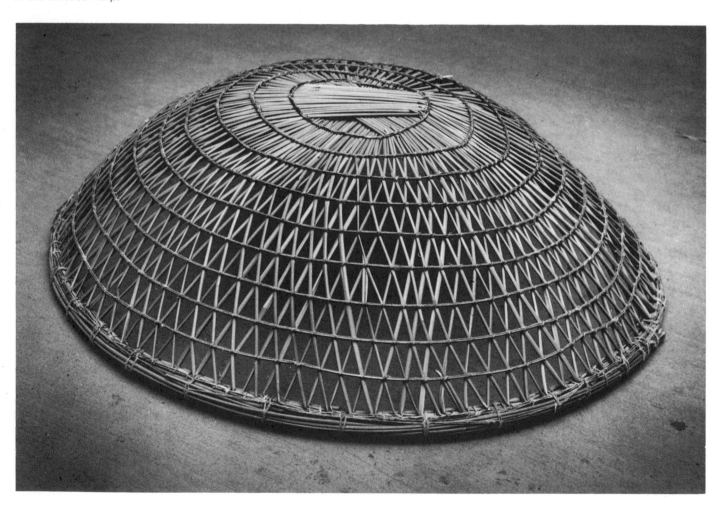

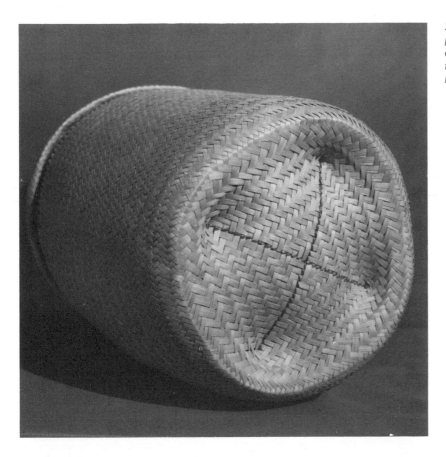

213. *Plaited palm basket, Mexico. The initial plaiting is held with stitching. At the base the elements are double. Where the sides start, the layers can be seen separating to provide more elements for the plaiting.*

214. *Another view of plaited palm basket, Mexico. The rim is rolled over so no rough ends are exposed.*

215. Coil basket, Pakistan. The center is a square of plaiting around which the foundation starts to spiral. Bits of cloth and metal foil are occasionally laid under the binder.

An entire basket can seem to be no more than the inevitable elaboration and development of the center configuration. Of such importance is the start—so interesting in the design of a basket—that starts have been almost overemphasized in the analysis of basketry. Charts of basic starts, along with charts of basic weaves, frequently accompany exhibitions of basketry, while other aspects of the construction are neglected. Familiar drawings show how the elements overlap or penetrate each other at the center of the base, how the "button" is devised at the center of a coil basket. It is a shock in studying baskets further to discover that the basketry process doesn't always start at the center of the base; that in fact many baskets start at the border and work to the base, or start at the handle, or start at one side and work across to the other side. And the process of making baskets can sometimes end not at the top, or bottom, or even one side or the other, but somewhere in the middle.

216. Twined basket, northwestern Washington. Coarse ribbons of bark appear at the center. They are split to form narrower warps for a wickerwork base before the twining starts on the sides.

Of lesser visual interest than the center, but critical to the construction process, is the point where the radiating stakes move from the horizontal plane of the base to the vertical of the sides. This abrupt change in direction is avoided in the Andaman Island basket by making the whole a continuous curve. But the basket has no base to sit on. Except in the shallowest platter baskets, a base implies a positive change of direction. This change strains the elements, which tend to crush or break or weaken at this point. The softer the curve as the stakes rise from the base to the sides, the less well-defined the change in direction, the easier on the stakes.

The smaller Andaman Island baskets show the soft curve at the base rather than an energetic upward-springing curve coming from a well-defined base. The baskets appear soft, flexible, malleable, sagging, as though from the weight of the contents. They are like gloves which have taken the shape of their wearer's hands. The baskets seem to have been formed by the contents and use, rather than by the controlling hands of the maker during the construction process. As in the large Andaman Island basket, areas of the stakes are left exposed at the border, declaring the nature of the stake elements which until this point show primarily as ribs encased by wefts. This open space is provided for convenience in tying something across the top to keep the contents from falling out. The observer who looks through the exposed stakes, which stand roughly parallel to each other but tip slightly, sees moiré patterns. The moirés continually shift as the observer changes his vantage point or as the basket moves before him. The activity seems generated from outside the modest, sagging baskets. These constant modifications, these fortuitous changes, so determined by external forces, are consistent with the total malleable, plastic appearance.

To refer again to the point in a basket where the stakes change direction to become the side walls, sometimes, as in the Yugoslavian basket described earlier, the initial radiating spokes are selected especially to provide a firm, durable base even though they are incapable of performing the necessary sharp bending to become side walls. A standard practice then, when the base is complete, is to cut off all the radiating spokes at the point where the direction must change, and replace them with others able to perform this feat. The new stakes are placed alongside the original ones, with a stake inserted on each side of the old stake. The base then appears as an entity separate from the side walls, partly because a positive change in direction occurs, partly because a change in material may be evident, and partly because the number of stakes has been suddenly increased, which influences the size of the stitches and therefore the appearance of the surface.

When the original stakes are bent upward to form the sides, the process requires the greatest care, often involving special dampening of the stakes and then sharply bending them with a small pliers. The inner part of the resulting bend shows a compression and broadening of the element, while the outer part of the curve appears stretched.

Frequently at this point of change in direction a sort of structural reinforcement is achieved by special twining techniques—as, for instance, through the use of three-strand twining when previously only two-strand twining had been used. The wefts pack closer together and form a thicker layer covering the stakes. Sometimes, too, this point in the construction is emphasized by a decorative use of materials—changes of color, weave, size of elements—similar to that which so often occurs at the border.

In some baskets, usually trays, the problem of establishing radiating spokes which must bend to form the side walls is avoided entirely by using a flat piece of wood as a base, with perforations around the edge for inserting the vertical stakes. The base is then not basketry at all. The sides are able to rise at right angles from the wooden base.

What the Andaman Islanders achieve with the stakes of their temporary baskets is the skeleton of a basket. The shape of the basket is pretty well established by the stakes alone. This is common to many baskets, both temporary and permanent. Skeletons are made from relatively strong and resistant materials such as cane, reeds, willow rods, and even wire. The final shape is set by this skeleton. Into such a frame the more delicate and pliable elements are interwoven, primarily to fill up the openings. The fillers can be inserted in any order, and in decorative and fanciful arrangements.

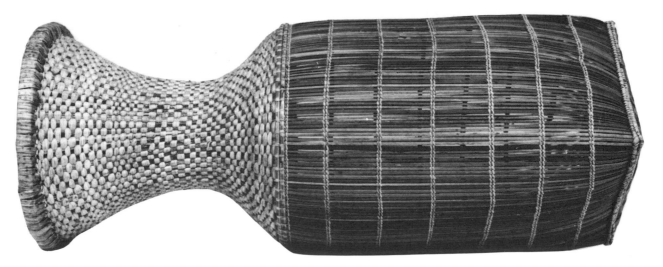

218. Another view of plaited and twined basket, Suku, Congo, Africa. At the mouth the elements are again brought together, and shaped with wickerwork.

219. Detail of plaited basket, Philippine Islands (see Fig. 148). A heavy strip of bamboo is carved into a crude hook and held in a hoop shape by a heavy stitch.

But in much basketry the shape is not established before the weft is inserted but is instead created throughout the process from an interaction of stakes and wefts. The wefts participate in the shaping of the basket. The work progresses slowly from the center of the bottom, row upon row, with the shape of the basket being constantly determined as the work progresses, by how tightly or how loosely the weft is entered, by the increase or decrease of the number of stakes, by changes in size and flexibility of the weft, etc. The curves of the basket are created throughout the process. The basketmaker continually controls the developing shape. When the Andaman Islanders force the reeds directly to the border, the reeds assume their own curves, which vary slightly from one reed to the next and are not modified by subsequent processes. The weft is neither supporting nor controlling the shape and holding the stakes in a precise position, but is filling in the curves already created. The relationship of stakes and weft differs basically in the different constructional approaches.

The distinctions in basketry regarding the functions of stakes and weft are like those in the art of weaving. While some wefts in cloth are only stuffing, filling in the openings between the warps, and other wefts exist only for their decorative quality, still other wefts are structural: without them the cloth would not exist.

The border, which terminates the basket shape, is usually also the termination of the basketry process. But with the temporary Andaman Island baskets, and the Greek melon-shaped basket, construction of the border occurs early in the process. The border has different meanings for the basket and for its maker, according to the method of construction, just as the weft has different meanings according to whether it is primarily a filler cutting down the size of the openings, or whether it is shape-determining.

To anyone who attempts basketry, the border when it terminates the process may seem even more remarkable than the start, more challenging to skill and ingenuity and artistry and patience. For here *all* the elements are ended. At the start, a few elements can begin, with others added later, but at the termination all must end simultaneously. The border must provide an ending that is visually appropriate as well as secure and durable, for at this point the basket is especially subject to wear and destruction from handling and holding and bumping and from friction as objects are put in and taken out—as can be seen by observing any collection of old baskets. Rough ends cannot be left to scratch the hands of the user, or to catch on anything which might cause the fragile elements to tear. All manner of twinings, braidings, and bindings have been devised for borders, with reinforcements often added to strengthen the border or to make it rigid. And decorative details are often superimposed. Sometimes at the border the stakes are forced to

220. Koryak basket, Siberia. The rim of this soft twined basket is reinforced with a wide strip of leather. (Courtesy of the American Museum of Natural History)

221. *Twined basket, Bella Coola, Northwest Coast. The crossed warps are held together with twining. At the rim the twining is worked close together as a reinforcement.*

222. Another view of twined basket, Bella Coola, Northwest Coast. The base of the basket is simple plaiting. At the edge of the base the elements are split and held with a row of twining.

223. Another view of plaited basket, Hopi, Arizona (see Fig. 156). The plaited elements are bent over a heavy hoop and held down with a row of twining.

change their direction to move parallel to the wefts or to participate in complicated configurations designed not only to be decorative but to hold the cut ends secure and out of the way, out of sight. Often the stakes are bent completely back upon themselves and the weaving continues for a short distance, so that the raw ends, which would disintegrate from wear if they were left on the very edge, occur some distance below the edge of the border. Or the ends are rolled inside the weaving in ingenious manipulations of flexible fibers. Such solutions of course are determined by the nature of the materials—their ability to bend sharply or to roll into a tight curve. In plaiting, each element is often folded back individually and carefully worked back into the structure. Often the ends of the structural elements disappear so completely, so skillfully and ingeniously, that the observer is scarcely aware that a most difficult problem existed and was solved.

It would be comfortable to subscribe to a scale of standards in basketry, to feel sure which method is the truest expression of the art, which approach or material represents the essence of basketry. Some people feel that the coil method of basketry construction is more truly sewing, that a wooden base with basketry sides is an evasion of primary basketry problems, and that "ware made from veneering" is a sort of desecration.

Applying to basketry the criteria which have prevailed in weaving, it might seem that ideally the basketmaking should start at the base and end at the border; the elements should all be structural; the shapes should arise from the interaction of stakes and wefts throughout the process; patterns and textures should be the result of materials and their structural organization rather than from superstructural additions; and the method of construction should be clearly expressed in the basket's appearance. Anyone trained in Bauhaus design theory, upon reading that in Oceania baskets are sometimes started not at the base and worked upward, but at the top border and worked downward, and that when some of these baskets are finished, the observer, even after careful examination, cannot tell where the basket was started since the various edges are left with the irregularities generally associated with the ending, might be inclined to question the process. But right and wrong are obscure in an ancient art that cannot even be adequately defined.

226. Unfinished basket, Yurok, northern California. All the loose weft ends have been left inside the basket, to be scraped off with a sharp tool.

THE PROCESS

10

Baskets are naturally thought of as hand products, the results of finger manipulation alone. The aborigines of the Andaman Islands use their feet to start a basket. They scoop out an indentation in the earth and lay the starting rods across this. Then they press a heel on the starting center so both hands are free to manipulate the extending elements. Such a use of the feet for holding work in place or in tension increases immeasurably the craftsman's potential for manipulating with his hands. Two hands are more than twice as effective as one hand. But beyond that, the process becomes more than finger manipulation; the body is involved more directly and completely.

Although large baskets are often started with the help of the feet, the use of the feet is not really common in basketmaking, and is of considerably less importance than in weaving or ceramics. The feet can be useful in only a short part of the basketry process, helping at the difficult time when the elements which will become stakes have not yet been firmly established in relationship to each other. As wefts are added, the position of each stake becomes secure, until finally the starting elements of the basket can be simultaneously held and manipulated by the hands.

Making a large basket can appear to be as physical an exercise as is the ceramic forming. Okey tells how the English willow basketmakers worked in a stooping position; for the apprentice, learning to work in this painfully exhausting position was known as "taking the backbone out." James, also, has described this physical aspect of the process of making large baskets in nineteenth-century England. The basketmaker stood in the center of his basket and bent over double to add to it. This is exactly like the ancient technique still used by coil potters of Persia who stand inside the large pots to build up the walls until the workers are virtually enclosed within their own constructions.

The use in basketmaking of parts of the body other than the hands is usually not so apparent or dramatic as the anchoring of the work with the heel. Yet the position of the basketmaker's body in relation to his work must constantly change. Each different aspect of the process—the creating of an inward curve or an outward curve or a rim—requires its own position of arms and hands, as well as of the torso itself. Furthermore, the increasing three-dimensional form of the basket constantly requires different ways of holding. Sometimes the basketmaker may hold the work out in space, and then as the basket increases, he may support it against his thigh, or surround and hold it with his arms.

Weavers with primitive backstrap looms use their bodies to control the tension of their warps by leaning forward or backward. The exercise of this control is often imperceptible to the observer and is performed almost unconsciously by the weaver. Similar delicate adjustments of body position are made by the basketmaker, and are just as imperceptible to the observer.

Clay being formed on the potter's wheel is spectacularly plastic. The potter can appear to be poised like an especially attentive observer while the clay moves and changes, searching for its own form, which it achieves

227. *Basketmaker from the Peruvian jungle.*

through trial and error. Much later the fluid material is transformed through firing into something immutable and remarkably permanent. Throwing clay on a wheel is an energetic, vigorous process. The physical endeavor of the potter, involving his whole body, is apparent in the wedging, centering, and raising of the clay. Finally, when only the tips of his fingers are controlling the form as it spins, he exerts—no matter how deceptively simple it may appear—his entire body to hold the fingers poised steadily and precisely in space.

Glass, like clay, can seem to change form of its own volition. In glassblowing, tools so separate the material from the craftsman that anyone watching must frequently concentrate on either the glass or the craftsman, rather than both simultaneously. Each seems to move independently. The relationship between the movements of both is fully evident only to an experienced observer. While the glass seems to move freely with a life of its own, the worker appears to put on a performance, dramatic and exhibitionistic. At the same time there is about the process a sense of constant pressure, the necessity to move at precise moments or to lose everything. Helpers are often essential.

By contrast, basketry never seems to develop by itself. The basketmaker never seems to be an observer, or to be in any way separated from his materials, or to be a performer. Rather he appears to be involved with manipulating his materials in a trancelike reverie, unaware of his surroundings or any audience. He sits quietly, calm and concentrated. Basketry is an inward process involving only a single individual. The worker's eyes or the tips of his fingers are always appraising the form developing from the manipulation. The point of construction is always perceived in relation to the portion already constructed and, somehow, in relation to the portion ahead which has not even been started. The concentration is expressed in the basketmaker's hands, to which all the rest of his being seems subsidiary. The fingers are constantly moving, working the materials to his will. The hand has not been extended by tools; no mechanism intervenes between the basketmaker and the basket; no separation implied or actual exists between the worker and his materials. They, the worker and the materials, seem a self-sufficient functioning unit.

The plastic nature of the materials is scarcely apparent to anyone but the basketmaker himself. To the observer the materials appear unresponsive, something to be pushed and forcibly held by knots and other constructional devices. Indeed, they seem recalcitrant and resisting. Yet the basketmaker continually senses a plasticity, a potential in each material for assuming new form. The plastic nature of basketry is something to be experienced, not observed. Perhaps if the process were filmed in very fast motion or photographed at time intervals, like the films of buds miraculously opening into flowers, the plastic nature would be clear. Such a revelation, however, would be achieved at too great an expense, for it would eliminate the essential time element, the basketmaker's awareness of regularly repeated movements in time, with the units of construction becoming units of time.

A remarkable quality of many baskets is the absolute regularity of spacing of the elements and the precise repetition of the stitches. In weaving, which is marked by similar regularity, the loom is equipped with a reed that keeps the warps evenly spaced throughout the piece. This regularity of spacing in weaving, maintained by the reed, continues unchanged. In basketry the regularity of spacing and intervals, the number of units, must change from weft row to weft row as the basket's shape increases or decreases.

The human potential for repeating movements identically, and for making the slightest modification in the movement and then repeating the modified movement identically, is beyond belief. The basketmaker does not calculate and measure to establish and maintain the equal spacing. The regularity results from the relative uniformity of his prepared materials, and the regularity of his movements. Each stake is responding to the same pressures as each other stake, and responding in the same ways. Thus, without equipment such as a spacing reed, the excellent craftsman produces baskets which show what we can think of only as something measured—what we have come to consider to be machine-like regularity.

The cylindrical form emerges from the basketry process about as inevitably as it does on the potter's wheel. The cylinder, like the regular spacing, results naturally from the process performed. Just as the potter's wheel when skillfully used encourages symmetry and inhibits asymmetry, the processes of basketmaking when skillfully practiced result in symmetry, so much so that asymmetry must be accomplished almost *against* the process, as an act of imposition of the craftsman's will.

Basketry is self-sufficient. Each basket establishes its own unit of measure according to the dimension of the materials being worked. Materials are never made to adapt, as they so frequently are in weaving, to arbitrary divisions of inches. The unit of measure is in the work itself, never imposed from some other system.

The continuous length of the elements in other textile processes, like the continuous nature of their products, has much to do with their susceptibility to mechanization. Throughout the long history of textiles, improvements in weaving have been paralleled by improvements in the production of yarns. The length of the elements and the size of the woven product gradually came into relation to the machine rather than to the individual craftsman, who, of course, was gradually eliminated.

Weaving became separated from human scale in another way. As skill in the manipulation of materials increased, yarns became finer, until they were so fine that hundreds could lie side by side in an inch of warp. When woven they were no longer distinguishable as individual elements. The stepped geometric patterns, considered typical of woven patterns, with the size of the steps determined by the dimension of the individual yarns—so apparent in weaving with coarse elements and similarly apparent in basketry—could be replaced by smooth curves, which were built of steps so small in scale that the eye no longer apprehended the steps but saw the flowing curves which could be no more than implied by coarser materials.

Along with the development of fine elements in weaving came devices for handling them. Woven constructions could become infinitely complex. The exact nature of the constructions became as imperceptible as the individual yarns. All sense of the interaction of elements to create the cloth disappeared. The curved forms, the appearance and disappearance of color seemed liberated from the traditional limitations of weaving. It is sometimes difficult to distinguish a woven pattern from a knit or printed pattern from any distance—the sense of structure creating pattern is lost.

In a brief statement about weaving as modern design, Edgar Kaufmann, Jr., stated that "now as always, the greatest delight a fabric can give comes from structure, the way threads support one another to create a cloth." In many modern textiles the perceptibility of threads supporting one another has given way to other textile delights. Handweavers are trying to restore the structural sense to weaving by increasing the dimension of the yarns, by simplifying woven structures, and by eliminating all superstructural elements and all concealing linings.

Basketry has never lost its elemental delight; it has retained the very qualities which many modern weavers are trying to restore to weaving. The materials, the process, and the product have always remained in immediate and direct relationship to the range of the basketmaker's hands and arms. The scale of the materials, even though some have been described by their preparers as "like threads," has continued within human perception. Individual elements can easily be traced as they perform the various configurations in the basketry structure.

One aspect alone in basketry has lost its human scale. This is the kind of quantity production in which a craftsman produces thousands of identical baskets in succession, rapid beyond belief. Such production is in scale with the machine. The basketmaker is not competing with a machine-made basket, for such a product does not exist. Instead he is competing with the bounty of the machine, of all the machines of the twentieth century. It is machine production by hand, a curious and tragic aberration of the modern world. To watch a craftsman making baskets in such quantity is to marvel at the human capacity for precise and incredibly rapid regular movements. At the same time that it seems undeniably marvelous, it seems funny, sad, and degrading. Like the product, the movements suggest the machine more than they suggest one's concept of man and the actions appropriate to him. Only at this moment does one feel that perhaps this textile process, like weaving and knitting, should have been mechanized.

CONCLUSION

At first the division of baskets into permanent and temporary appears reasonable. Then the distinction seems less clear but still a relief from the usual classification of baskets according to technique. Finally the categories seem not only invalid but deceptive and downright mischievous.

Because we have direct evidence that hunting-gathering people made baskets as they needed them and then threw them away—simple, direct, rough-and-ready constructions—we can more easily associate baskets with neolithic or late paleolithic times. In temporary baskets we feel we can discern the very beginnings of basketry. We can link such temporary baskets with ground and polished tools; with arrowheads, celts, daggers, battle axes; with the clumsy brutes in dioramas. We can allow these ancestors the incipient baskets, not "real" baskets. We can avoid acknowledging the magnificent skill and technical development of these early men, especially in a product which we still use.

The thought remains enchanting that the most temporary baskets, in their directness and simplicity, are the purest expression of the basket art. Their continuing use in hunting-gathering activities seems to place them close to the first baskets, as duplicates of the prototypes from the time of the first hunter-gatherers. The simple converting of natural materials seems to be the essence of basketry.

But then, in studying the most permanent baskets, the time element appears. The process of making a basket in five minutes is fundamentally different from the process of making a basket over many months. Time becomes an ingredient; the basketmaking process induces not only meditation and contemplation, but an unusual awareness of time, a measuring of time, a manipulation of time, a celebration, an observation. The units of construction become units of time measured. Basketry, like the other textile arts, becomes a time experience.

If we could forget the familiar definitions and classifications of the arts and look afresh at basketmaking, not concentrating so much on the product and its relation to the process, basketmaking might seem to be more akin to music than to the visual arts, more of a time experience than a space experience, more concerned with the time aspect of manipulating materials than the spatial aspects. Basketmaking might then be thought of as an experience in dividing and organizing time, breaking time into modular units determined by the basketmaker, units more complex than minutes and seconds, to be arranged in sequences and patterns. Basketmaking might be a sort of clock, not a measuring device, but something devised by man to enforce an awareness, a savoring, of time through its arbitrary division into rhythmic units.

When a product such as a basket results from a process we are inclined to assume that the result was the reason that the process was performed. Any statements regarding joy in the doing are not truly convincing against the solid evidence of the result.

Yet it would be impossible to ascertain whether a basketmaker wants a basket primarily or the involvement in the process primarily—and then to what extent the performance of the process is kinaesthetic satisfaction, and to what extent it is the pleasure of handling materials, bending them to an ordered set of configurations or developing an idea through the materials—or whether the rhythmic repetition of movements is not significant as providing a means of experiencing time in ways usually associated with music.

While music is considered to be a time art by those who think in such terms, roles keep shifting. Such ambiguity, such merging and flowing in defiance of established classifications, perhaps would not be so upsetting were it not for the contemporary predilection for categories. While they are convenient, yet they direct and limit our comprehensions, our ways of viewing and dealing with the world's complexities. Often the played musical composition, like the basket, might be thought of as a by-product of an experience. The real essence of the musical composition might not reside in the sounds so much as in the appearance and distribution of marks on a sheet of paper. The composer's intelligence and ingenuity are apparent not so much in the listened-to music as visually in the score, which can be responded to perhaps best without being transcribed, even mentally, into sounds.

While the temporary baskets lack the time-measuring repetition, the permanent baskets lack the direct transformation of a natural form into a man-made object. Both essences are in the process, perhaps to be experienced almost intuitively in the result.

Presumably, paintings of the abstract expressionists communicate to the observer the drama of the process—the brush spreading the paint, the splashing of color, the resistance of the canvas surface against the brush. The dynamics of the act are expressed in the product, and communicated through it. But the product of basketry, the basket, does not so communicate, perhaps because the deliberate manipulation is not within the experience of most viewers, and certainly is not so obvious an expression of a gesture, a movement, an act. The baskets which are most the products of such a deep time experience may be the most difficult to respond to except as a sort of respect or even wonder for the precision and neatness of the execution. Such baskets seem peculiarly inward and introspective, personal expressions not in the sense of symbols and motifs which would have recognition or emotional value only for the artist, but a record of personal experience—the basket is the record of the experience.

In the paintings of the abstract expressionists, the artist's gestures and his vigorous direct handling of his materials are thought of as being experienced vicariously by those viewing the completed painting. Yet communication of the experience to the viewer may be a secondary consideration as far as the artist is concerned. In a world consisting more and more of spectators, we are enchanted with the idea of "communication" as a substitute for direct experience. The artist communicates his emotions and responses to an audience, as though the communication were of more significance than the experience itself, as though the experience existed for the communication. The painting may be only a by-product of the experience of manipulating paint on a canvas. While it may provide the audience with a vicarious experience in manipulating paint, the depth of the vicarious experience is limited by the depth of the audience's previous direct experience. Watching a travelog is no more to be confused with traveling than watching a riot on television is to be confused with being a participant or even a bystander.

Perhaps today baskets are little able to communicate much about the basketmaking experience because few can receive the message. Yet when a person says, upon looking at a basket or any other textile, "Think of the time it took to make it," he may be doing more than merely illuminating (as the artist who made the object may interpret the remark) the distorted values which are part of the detestable illness of the century, that anything which takes time is not worth bothering with. It has become essential to feel a pressure of time, to reject anything which requires an abundance of time. And with such a rejection of doing ourselves, we reject any full appreciation of what others are doing or have done. Yet by feeling "time" when he confronts a piece of quilting or embroidery or lacemaking or basketry, the viewer may be close to the essence of the art.

BIBLIOGRAPHY

Franz Boas, *Primitive Art* (New York: Dover Publications, Inc., 1955).

Peter H. Buck, *Arts and Crafts of Hawaii* (Honolulu: Bishop Museum Press, 1957).

The Material Culture of the Cook Islands (New Plymouth, N.Z.: Thomas Avery & Sons, Ltd., 1927).

F. J. Christopher, *Basketry* (New York: Dover Publications, Inc., 1952).

Ciba Review, Basle

"The Essentials of Handicrafts and the Craft of Weaving Among Primitive Peoples," No. 30, Feb. 1940.

"Bamboo," 1969/3.

Viva Cooke and Julia Sampley, *Palmetto Braiding and Weaving* (Peoria: The Manual Arts Press, 1947).

Charles Crampton, *Rush Baskets and Mats,* Dryad Leaflet No. 112 (Leicester: Dryad Handicrafts).

Grace M. Crowfoot, "Textiles, Basketry and Mats," in *A History of Technology,* edited by Charles Singer et al. (Oxford: Clarendon Press, 1958).

Thomas Kingston Derry and Trevor I. Williams, *A Short History of Technology* (New York: Oxford University Press, 1961).

Philip Drucker, *Indians of the Northwest Coast* (New York: McGraw-Hill, 1955).

Irene Emery, *The Primary Structures of Fabrics* (Washington, D.C., The Textile Museum, 1966).

R. J. Forbes, *Studies in Ancient Technology,* Vol. IV (Leiden: E. J. Brill, 1956).

R. J. Forbes and E. J. Dijksterhuis, *A History of Science and Technology,* Vol. I (Baltimore, Md.: Penguin Books, 1963).

Willowdean Chatterson Handy, *Handcrafts of the Society Islands,* (Honolulu: The Museum, 1927).

Mary Lois Kissell, *Basketry of the Papago and Pima,* Anthropological Papers of the American Museum of Natural History, Vol. XVII, Part IV, New York, 1916.

J. Merritt Matthews, *The Textile Fibers* (New York: John Wiley & Sons, 1924).

Lila M. O'Neale, *Yurok-Karok Basket Weavers,* University of California Publications in American Archaeology and Ethnology, Vol. 32, No. 1 (Berkeley: University of California Press, 1932).

Weaving, The Arts of the Maori, Instructional Booklet, Department of Education, Arts and Crafts Branch, Wellington, New Zealand, 1968.

Margaret M. Wheat, *Survival Arts of the Paiutes* (Reno, Nevada: University of Nevada Press, 1967).

TEXT REFERENCES

Page 9. *Dictionary of American Biography,* edited by Dumas Malone, Vol. IX (New York: Charles Scribner's Sons, 1932), p. 577.

Page 9. George Wharton James, *Indian Basketry, and How to Make Indian and Other Baskets* (New York: Henry Malkan, 1909), p. 15.

Page 9. Otis Tufton Mason, *Indian Basketry, Studies in Textile Art without Machinery* (New York: Doubleday, Page & Co., 1904), p. viii and p. 4.

Page 9. Gertrude Ashley and Mildred Ashley, *Raffia Basketry as a Fine Art* (Deerfield: Published by the Authors, 1915).

Page 10. Thomas Okey, *An Introduction to the Art of Basket-making* (London: Sir I. Pitman & Sons, Ltd., 1912).

Page 16. Mills College Art Gallery, *California Indian Basketry* (1967).

Page 17. Lidio Cipriani, *The Andaman Islanders* (New York: F.A. Praeger, 1966), p. 39.

Page 17. A.R. Radcliffe-Brown, *The Andaman Islanders* (The Free Press of Glencoe, 1964).

Page 30. Walter E. Roth, "Some Technical Notes from the Pomeroon District, British Guiana," *Journal of the Royal Anthropological Institute of Great Britain and Ireland,* Vol. 41 (1911).

Page 30. James S. Ackerman and Rhys Carpenter, *Art and Archeology* (Englewood Cliffs, New Jersey: Prentice-Hall, 1963), p. 141.

Page 46. Hideyuki Oka, *How to Wrap Five Eggs* (New York: Harper and Row, 1967).

Page 46. H. Krafft, *A Travers le Turkestan Russe* (Paris: Hachette et Cie, 1902).

Page 49. *Peasant Art in Italy,* edited by Charles Holme (London: The Studio, Ltd. 1913), p. 41.

Page 52. Masataka Ogawa, *The Enduring Crafts of Japan, 33 Living National Treasures* (New York, Tokyo: Walker/Weatherhill, 1968), p. 194.

Page 52. C. Gadsen Porcher, "Basketry of the Aleutian Islands," *The Basket,* No. 2, Vol. 2 (April 1904), pp. 67 ff.

Page 99. Herbert Read, *Art and Industry* (New York: Harcourt, Brace and Co., 1938), p. 95.

Page 105. Luther Weston Turner, *The Basket Maker* (New York: Atkinson, Mentzer & Co. 1909).

Page 191. Edgar Kaufmann, Jr., *What is Modern Design?* (New York: The Museum of Modern Art, 1950), p. 16.

INDEX